THE MAN YOU'RE CALLED TO BE

A 100-Day Journey To Power, Clarity & Rebuilding Your Life

BY ANTHONY D BRICE

The Impower Group, LLC.

The Man You're Called to Be
Copyright © 2025 by The Impower Group, LLC.
All rights reserved.

No part of this book may be copied, stored, or shared in any format—electronic, mechanical, photocopying, recording, or otherwise—without prior written permission from the publisher, except for brief quotations in reviews or articles.
Published by The Impower Group
Fort Mill, SC

ISBN: 979-8-9887656-2-2 (Paperback)
Printed in the United States of America

Library of Congress Control Number: 2025906194

For permissions, bulk orders, or inquiries, contact: anthony@anthonydbrice.com

TABLE OF CONTENT

Dedication — iv

Introduction — v

How to Use This Book — xvi

Pillar 1 — 01
Face It. Own It. Move Forward
(Days 1–15)

Pillar 2 — 40
Resilience Is Built, Not Given
(Days 16–29)

Pillar 3 — 78
Step Into the Man You Were Built to Be
(Days 30–45)

Pillar 4 — 118
Owning Your Power
(Days 46-73)

Pillar 5 — 190
Forged in the Fire
(Days 74–80)

Pillar 6 — 212
The Legacy You Live, Not Just Leave
(Days 81–100)

Conclusion	265
Acknowledgements	272
About the Author	276

DEDICATION

To the man who's carried the weight of expectations but never felt truly seen.

To the man who's sacrificed, fought, and endured—and still wonders if it was enough.

To the man who's ready to break cycles, reclaim his power, and rise into the man he was born to be—

This book is for you.

INTRODUCTION

THE WEIGHT YOU CARRY

Before you even get out of bed, life is already swinging. It doesn't wait for you to be ready—it just comes at you. Work deadlines. Family expectations. Bills piling up. It's relentless. And somewhere in the chaos, you start to wonder: Am I doing enough? Am I enough?

Society tells you to man up, to tough it out, to figure it out alone. But nobody gives you a blueprint for carrying that weight without it breaking you. Every man carries a burden the world will never see. But real strength? It's not in pretending you've got it—it's in facing it head-on.

Strength isn't just about how much you can carry. It's about knowing when to adjust the load, when to ask for support, and when to stand firm in who you are. The pressure isn't just mental—it's physical. It tightens your chest. Sits heavy in your gut. Stiffens your shoulders.

You're expected to be the rock, the provider, the protector. But what happens when the weight gets too heavy? What happens when the cracks start to show?

Pretending you're fine doesn't make the load lighter. It just makes you lonelier.

Maybe you're on autopilot, handling business. To everyone else, you look like you've got it together. But inside? There's a storm you can't calm. And the longer you ignore it, the worse it gets.

What you don't deal with, deals with you. That stress? It lives in your body. Robs your focus. Wrecks your sleep. You can bury it, but it always finds its way back—and when it does, it hits harder.

I know that fight because I've lived it. Growing up with an incarcerated father and a single mother in a neighborhood where survival was the only goal, stress wasn't something you talked about. It was just part of life.

I thought silence was strength. That handling everything on my own made me a man. But holding it all in doesn't make you strong—it makes you exhausted.

You weren't built to break. Your setbacks don't define you—your fight back does. Strength isn't about carrying everything alone. It's about knowing when to put the weight down, when to ask for help, and when to stop running from what's really going on inside.

Facing what's real doesn't make you weak—it makes you dangerous in all the right ways. Because a man who knows himself can't be shaken.

Imagine what would shift if you stopped pretending you were fine and gave yourself permission to breathe. Not just for yourself, but for the people who count on you.

What if you allowed yourself to rest, to connect, to stop believing you have to do it all alone? Every man deserves to feel whole—not just to survive, but to live. This book isn't about perfection—it's about progress.

Every challenge, every setback, every moment of doubt is shaping you into something stronger.

You are not alone in this. We're in this together—a brotherhood of men choosing to break the silence, lift each other up, and redefine strength on our own terms. The man who keeps going, even when no one is watching, is the man who builds an unshakable foundation.

So, leave the masks behind and step into something different—something real. A life where strength and self-awareness don't compete but coexist. A life where your journey becomes the foundation of the legacy you're building.

You've carried this weight long enough. Now, it's time to take the next step.

THE WEIGHT MADE YOU

Every man has his battles. I've fought mine too.

The pressure to measure up. The weight of expectations that never let up. The doubt that whispers, Are you enough?

Your story might not look exactly like mine, but struggle speaks the same language. And if there's one thing I want you to take from this—it's this: Your past doesn't define you. But what you do next will.

My father was incarcerated for over 30 years, leaving me to navigate manhood without his presence. My mother had me when she was just 19. She raised me with the help of my grandmother and a community of strong women who wrapped me in resilience, love, and faith. They taught me what it meant to keep going—no matter what.

But the world I grew up in wasn't easy. My neighborhood wasn't all bad, but the hustle, the grind, the choices people made to survive—it all made sense. Still, deep down, I knew I wanted something different.

I remember one of the few times my father was present outside of prison. It was my elementary school's field day. I got heat exhaustion and passed out, and he carried me to a tent to cool down. I can still feel the weight of his arms holding me—the rare comfort of having my father there when I needed him. But that moment was fleeting—just like his presence in my life.

The next time I saw him, it was at my grandmother's funeral. He was shackled, flanked by armed deputies. One moment, he was my protector. The next, he was a prisoner.

Moments like that leave a mark. They show you the gaps, the pain, and the lessons you don't even realize you're learning until years later.

INTRODUCTION

But something shifted.

I saw something—a glimpse of the man I wasn't yet, but knew I could be. I was eight years old, standing in my grandmother's living room, staring out the glass door. I caught my reflection—but it wasn't just me. I saw an older version of myself. I was in a business suit, standing in a downtown office, a city skyline behind me. It felt so real I stepped closer.

Then, the scene changed. I was surrounded—millions of people, their pain thick in the air. A woman in a headscarf reached out, her eyes heavy with sorrow. Without thinking, I reached into my chest and placed a ball of light in her palm. She smiled. Her tears turned to joy. More people came. I kept reaching, kept giving, until the vision faded, and I was back in that living room.

That vision became my promise. And maybe you've had one too—a moment, a whisper, a knowing that there's more for you. Hold onto it. Let it drive you forward.

That vision kept me grounded. It kept me away from the easy escapes that could've pulled me under. I didn't drink or use drugs because I couldn't afford to lose sight of what I'd seen. Even when life hit me hard—like in 2016, when the company I'd worked for shut down my location—I had to find my way.

Newly married. A new house. A newborn. I could've taken the demotion, but I bet on myself. Some nights, I made five bucks designing graphics. Some nights, I felt like I was failing. But I couldn't let the pressure break me.

So, when I talk about being stretched to the limit—trying to be the best father, husband, son, and man while constantly wondering if it's enough—I'm not speaking hypothetically.

I know the weight. I've carried it too. And that's why this book exists. Not to give you easy answers. Not to hand you clichés about "manning up." But to remind you that you're not alone. Together, we're not just breaking cycles—we're rewriting the definition of success and building a legacy that actually matters.

This isn't about quick fixes. It's about doing the real work—digging deep, rising up, and becoming the man you were built to be. This is our journey, and I'm honored to walk it with you.

Because everything you've been through wasn't meant to stop you—it was meant to shape you.

THE MESSAGE THAT BROKE THE SILENCE

On May 8, 2024, I shared a message that didn't just resonate—it roared. It was raw, real, and straight from the heart. No filters. No fluff. Just truth. I had no idea it would reach so many people. But what happened next made one thing clear: This message wasn't just heard—it was needed.

The response was staggering:

- Over 5 million views
- 307,000+ likes
- 7,000+ comments
- 663,000+ shares

But this wasn't about numbers. It was about men finally feeling seen.

The comments poured in:

"You have no idea how much I needed this."

"I've been feeling lost, unwanted—like I'm fighting this battle alone. Thank you for reminding me that I'm not."

These weren't just words on a screen. They were battle cries. Proof of a weight too heavy to carry alone.

INTRODUCTION

Because from the time we're boys, we're told the same story:

Your worth is in what you provide.

Your value is measured in money, status, and how tough you look.

Your emotions? A liability. Bury them. Numb them. Ignore them. Or else.

That kind of pressure doesn't just weigh on you—it changes you. It shapes your decisions. It controls how you show up. It affects how you love, how you lead, and how you see yourself.

But strip all of that away, and what do most of us really want?

To be good men. To be present. To be fathers, partners, brothers, and leaders who show up fully, pour into others, and leave something real behind.

And yet—we're told to carry it all alone. To suffer in silence. To put on the mask and pretend we're fine.

But hear me: what you don't deal with, will deal with you.

That stress? It doesn't just live in your head. It settles in your body—your chest, your gut, your sleep. Until one day, it spills out onto the people you love.

This isn't some distant issue. It's real. It's happening now. And that's exactly why this book exists.

Not to lecture you. Not to hand out clichés.

But to walk with you.

This is a conversation, not a sermon. A brotherhood, not a manual. A call to rise—not just read.

I'm not above the struggle—I'm in it with you. I know what it feels like to question your worth. To wonder if you're ever going to measure up. But I also know this: Every challenge you've faced is a chance to grow into the man you're called to be.

We'll walk through the hard truths, the setbacks, and the victories. Not just to survive them—but to rise because of them.

Let this be the moment everything shifts. The moment you stop carrying this alone. You've held the weight long enough.

Now it's time to take the first step forward.

This isn't about waiting. It's about rising.

The challenge isn't knowing—it's doing.

Are you ready?

THE CHOICE IS YOURS

This book isn't here to fix you—because you're not broken. Life's challenges are real, and they're heavy. But so are you. This isn't theory. It's not fluff. It's real talk and real tools for the road ahead.

We're going to dig into the things that matter most:

- How to carry responsibility without losing yourself
- How to face self-doubt head-on
- How to find purpose when life feels like chaos

Imagine waking up and knowing you can handle whatever the day throws at you. Not because life got easier, but because you got stronger. Because you've built the mindset, the resilience, and the habits to keep moving—even when it's hard.

I remember a time when I wasn't sure I could. My account was low, my bills were high, and my confidence was shot. I sat in my car, gripping the wheel, wondering if I had what it took to make it.

Doubt sat in my chest like a weight I couldn't lift. But instead of letting it crush me, I made one move. Just one.

INTRODUCTION

One phone call. One decision. One action.

And that's the key. Change doesn't come from waiting on a breakthrough—it comes from choosing to move, even if the step is small. Every win—no matter how quiet—is proof that you've got what it takes to face what's ahead.

You don't need the perfect moment. You need the next one. And this time, you're not walking alone.

There's a brotherhood of men out here choosing growth over silence, healing over hiding, purpose over pressure. We're not following that tired blueprint of what a man "should" be. We're building a new one—together.

And eventually, there comes a moment where staying the same is more painful than the fear of change. When the ache of standing still outweighs the risk of moving forward.

That's the moment you step into your power.

Not the power the world talks about. Not titles, money, or applause. Real power. The kind that comes from knowing who you are, standing on what you believe, and choosing to rise—even when life is trying to knock you down.

So, ask yourself:

What dream have you buried?

What have you talked yourself out of because fear got louder than faith?

Stepping into your power doesn't require perfection. It just requires movement. It's about showing up. Falling forward. Learning as you go. It's about grit, not gloss. And getting up—every single time you fall.

The time isn't later.

It's now.

THE MAN YOU'RE CALLED TO BE

You're stronger than you think. More capable than you've been told. And no matter what you're facing, you don't have to face it alone.

The future you want isn't out of reach. It's waiting for you to move.

You don't need a plan. You need a step. No more waiting. No more hesitation.

It starts now. You're not waiting anymore—you're stepping into it.

Right now.

The man you're becoming starts with the choice you make today.

So, let's go—all in. No turning back.

INTRODUCTION

FOR THE ONES WHO SEE US

Challenge: If there's a woman in your life—someone who's stood by you, believed in you, or carried weight alongside you—I want you to do something.

In the next 24 hours, read this next section to her. Not through a screen. Not in a text. Read it from your own mouth, in your own voice. Because sometimes, the most powerful thing a man can do isn't just to show up—it's to speak.

Before we move forward, I want to acknowledge the women who may be reading this book for the men they care about. Whether you're a wife, a girlfriend, a mother, a sister, or a friend—your presence in our lives doesn't go unnoticed. Your belief in us—especially in the moments we struggle to believe in ourselves—matters more than you know.

Your patience.

Your support.

Your presence.

Some days, it's the only thing that keeps us standing.

This journey isn't just about men—it's about all of us. It's about building strength together. It's about understanding one another in a world that too often tells us to stay quiet, to carry it all alone, to never need anyone.

But the truth is, we grow because of the love, the grace, and the steady presence of the people who refuse to let us fall.

So to the women reading—or being read to—thank you.

Thank you for seeing us. For supporting us. For reminding us we're not alone. Your role in this story is bigger than you may ever know. Your belief in us fuels this journey more than we can say. And now—it's time for every man to choose to walk it.

That choice starts now.

The man you're becoming isn't waiting—he's already in you.

The only thing standing between you and him… is a decision.

No more hesitation. No more second-guessing.

It's time to step forward and claim him.

HOW TO USE THIS BOOK

This isn't a book you just read—it's a book you live through.

Every reflection in here is meant to challenge you, push you, and sharpen you into the man you were built to be. Real transformation doesn't happen from the outside in—it happens when you fully engage with the process. This journey is about presence, honesty, and action.

Here's how to get the most out of it:

1. READ ONE REFLECTION A DAY

This book is a daily journey—100 days of growth, clarity, and rebuilding from the inside out. Each reflection builds on the last, helping you unpack what's been weighing on you and step into your power. If something hits you hard, don't rush past it. Sit with it. Reread it. Journal. Talk it through with someone you trust. And if you miss a day? Don't quit. Life happens. Just pick up where you left off and keep moving.

2. APPLY THE ACTION CHALLENGES

Every reflection ends with an Action Challenge—a step designed to move you from thinking to doing. These aren't suggestions. They're part of the process. Change doesn't happen in your head—it happens in your habits. Some of these will stretch you. That's the point. Lean in. That's where growth lives. Track your progress. Write your responses. Reflect on how each step is shaping you.

3. BE HONEST WITH YOURSELF

This journey only works if you keep it real—with yourself. Some days will be heavy. Some entries will bring up things you've buried or ignored. That's okay. That's the work. The more truth you face, the more freedom you gain. Don't run from it. Rise through it.

4. ENGAGE WITH BROTHERHOOD

You were never meant to do this alone. The strongest men are the ones who know how to lean in, speak up, and grow together. If you can, go through this book with a brother, a mentor, or a trusted friend. Share what's hitting you. Talk through what's shifting. You'll be surprised how powerful it is to be seen and supported.

5. COMMIT TO THE PROCESS

You didn't get here overnight—and you won't rebuild overnight either. This is a process. Show up for it. Stay in it. Do the work. And if you do, you won't just change—you'll become more grounded, more focused, and more aligned than you've ever been.

This isn't about becoming someone else. It's about remembering who you've always been—and giving yourself permission to finally become him.

Let's get to work.

PILLAR 1

FACE IT. OWN IT. MOVE FORWARD

(DAYS 1–15)

Every transformation starts with one decision: to stop running and face where you are. Growth, purpose, and redefining manhood all begin with honesty—an unfiltered look at your reality. No more sweeping struggles under the rug. No more pretending the weight isn't heavy.

This phase is about stripping away the masks, stepping out of the shadows, and confronting what's been quietly breaking you. The world demands a lot from men—more than it gives in return. We're told to be the rock—the unshakable foundation everyone else leans on. But under that weight? Even rocks start to crack.

You've held it together for everyone else. Now, it's time to hold space for yourself.

Phase 1 is about breaking the silence that's been keeping you stuck. It's about rejecting the lie that men should suffer quietly. The stress. The fear. The silent battles no one else sees. They're real. They're heavy. But you were never meant to carry them alone.

This isn't about quick fixes or chasing perfection. It's about recognizing how the weight is affecting you—mentally, physically, emotionally—and making the choice to start lightening the load. Think about the nights you've lain awake, replaying the worries. Wondering if you're doing enough. If you are enough.

That's where we begin. Not with shame—but with truth.

This is your starting point. You'll see yourself in these reflections. You'll recognize your own quiet struggles in these pages. But more than that—you'll find your strength here.

I won't speak in theories. I'll walk with you through the hard truths, sharing my own battles and the lessons I had to learn the hard way. Because this isn't just about naming what's been weighing you down—it's about reclaiming what's yours.

Your peace.

Your direction.

Your power.

Take a deep breath. Acknowledge the weight without trying to outrun it. You don't need all the answers today. But you do need to choose to keep going.

You're not alone in this. This isn't just your journey—it's ours. A brotherhood of men choosing to rise together.

But before we move forward, we've got to confront what's been holding us back:

The weight we've been carrying.

Because you can't build something stronger if you're already breaking under the load.

DAY 1

LIGHTEN THE LOAD BEFORE IT BREAKS YOU DOWN

You wake up, and the weight is already there. The responsibilities. The expectations. The pressure that never lets up. It's always pressing, isn't it?

Burnout doesn't knock—it creeps in. One skipped meal. One sleepless night. One more time saying, "I'll deal with it later." And then even the simple stuff starts feeling heavy. You used to feel driven. Now it just feels like you're going through the motions.

I know this because I ignored the alarms. I told myself I was fine, even as the cracks started to show. I brushed off the exhaustion, the irritability, the way my body felt heavier every day. And then one day, my body called my bluff.

I ended up in the hospital.

That moment hit me hard. But it taught me something I've never forgotten: You either listen to your body, or your body will make you listen. You either sit down, or life will sit you down. Burnout doesn't ask for permission—it just takes over. And if you don't make changes now, the cost only gets higher.

You've been carrying it so long, you've convinced yourself it's normal. But it's not.

This isn't just about being tired. It's about the emotional and mental toll of pushing through without pause. The weight of expectations, the pressure to keep going no matter what—it doesn't just disappear.

It buries itself in your body, your mind, and the way you move through life.

Maybe you've felt it—the frustration creeping in. The way little things that never used to bother you now feel unbearable. The constant sense that you're running on fumes.

That's not normal. And it's not sustainable.

So, let's ask the hard question: When was the last time you really checked in with yourself? Have you been hoping the pressure would ease up on its own? Telling yourself you'll rest "when things calm down?"

They won't.

Admitting you need a moment to breathe isn't weakness. It's control. It's reclaiming your power before burnout takes it from you.

You're not weak for feeling this way—you're human. And you're not alone.

You weren't meant to carry it all—and you don't have to. Today is the first day you stop breaking for everyone else and start building for you.

ACTION CHALLENGE

Step 1: Identify the Strain. Write down three areas in your life where you feel most stretched thin. (Work? Relationships? Your own mental health?)

Step 2: Lighten the Load. Choose one of those areas and take an action today to reduce the weight.

Some examples:

- Delegate one task. (Pass something off instead of doing it all yourself.)
- Say no to something. (You don't have to take on everything.)
- Set a boundary. (Protect your time and energy.)

Strength isn't found in how much you can carry. It's in knowing when to stop, assess, and lighten the load so you can keep moving forward.

Because the man who chooses to move—even when the weight feels unbearable—is the man who refuses to break.

Your journey starts here.

DAY 2

TURN DOUBT INTO YOUR DRIVE

Every man knows that voice—the one that creeps in just when you're about to move.

"Are you sure you're good enough?"

"What if you fail?"

It's not always loud, but it lingers. It questions your every step.

But self-doubt doesn't have to be your enemy.

I remember finishing my first book. I poured everything into it—my time, my energy, my heart. But when it came time to publish, doubt showed up hard.

Would anyone read it? Would anyone care?

I almost didn't release it.

But I pushed through, and that book became a #1 release on Amazon its first week.

Now, I'm working on my seventh.

That moment taught me something I've never forgotten: Doubt doesn't mean stop. It means you're stepping into something that matters.

Doubt shows up when you're on the edge of growth. It doesn't visit people playing small—it finds the ones reaching for more. That uneasy feeling? It's a sign you're stepping into unfamiliar territory. Something bigger than where you've been.

So instead of letting it shut you down—use it.

What if, every time that voice said, "You can't", you answered with, "Watch me."

Doubt doesn't show up when you're standing still. It's a signal you're moving toward something real. Let it be fuel. Let it drive you. Let it remind you—you're built for what's next.

ACTION CHALLENGE

Step 1: Identify Your Doubt.

Think of one area in your life where self-doubt has been loud lately. (Work? A relationship? A personal goal?)

Write it down and ask yourself:

What's one thing I can do today to challenge this doubt?

Step 2: Take the Step.

Choose one action to push past the doubt:

- Speak up in a situation where you've been holding back.
- Begin something you've been putting off—send the email, make the call, take the first step.
- Write down a past win that proves you can do hard things.

Every small step you take chips away at doubt.

Progress doesn't need to be loud or flashy—it just needs to be consistent.

The more you move, the less power doubt has over you.

Keep going, and let your actions be the proof that doubt was wrong all along.

DAY 3

FREE YOURSELF FROM WHAT'S WEIGHING YOU DOWN

You wake up every day under the weight of expectations—those unspoken rules about what it means to be a man. Be the provider. Keep it together. Show no weakness.

These demands don't just pull you—they crush you. They steal your peace before the day even begins. And somewhere along the way, you started believing that the weight is what defines your worth.

But have you ever stopped to ask: Whose expectations are you carrying?

Are they yours—or borrowed from society, family, or someone who's never walked in your shoes?

That pressure to never slip, to never falter—that's not strength. That's a burden. And it comes with a cost. Sleepless nights. Tension in your body. That constant feeling like you're walking a tightrope.

It's not strength if it's breaking you.

Carrying it all doesn't make you stronger—it just wears you down.

I knew a man who lived by those rules. Never asked for help. Always held it in. Always played the strong one. He carried it all, never once considering that maybe... he didn't have to.

And then one day, his body made the choice for him.

Stress put him in the hospital—forced him to stop when he wouldn't stop himself.

That was his wake-up call. It doesn't have to be yours.

Strength isn't about shouldering everything alone. It's about knowing what's worth carrying—and what it's time to set down.

Imagine letting go of even one expectation that drains you.

Something you've outgrown. Something you never agreed to in the first place.

What would your life look like without that weight?

How much more energy could you pour into what actually matters?

ACTION CHALLENGE

Step 1: Drop the Dead Weight.

Write down one unrealistic or heavy expectation you've been carrying.

Then, ask yourself:

"How has this expectation held me back?"

Commit to one action to release its hold—say no, delegate a task, or take a break.

Step 2: Move for 15 Minutes.

Physical activity relieves stress and reinforces letting go.

Take a walk, hit the gym, or do pushups—move your body intentionally as a symbolic act of shedding the weight.

Choosing to release the weight doesn't make you selfish—it makes you wise.

Every man deserves to live on his own terms, free from the chains of expectations that don't align with who he truly is.

DAY 4

TAKE OFF THE MASK BEFORE IT BECOMES A CAGE

Most days, you step into the world wearing a mask—a version of yourself that says, "I'm good," even when you're drowning. That mask helps you get through conversations, responsibilities, and work without raising questions. It keeps things moving. It keeps people out.

But keeping it on comes at a cost. It disconnects you from the people who care. It distances you from your own truth. Over time, the mask stops being protection—and starts feeling like a cage you can't escape.

We wear these masks because we were taught to. "Stay strong." "Don't let them see you sweat." Somewhere along the way, we started believing the lie that vulnerability is weakness.

But the longer you hide, the lonelier you become.

I knew a guy who always played it cool. No matter what life threw at him, he acted like he had it all together. Never let on when he was struggling. Then life hit him with something he couldn't outrun—he lost someone close to him. And for the first time, he broke down in front of his boys.

He expected them to pull away. To judge him. To see him as soft. But instead, they pulled him in closer.

That moment changed everything for him. For the first time, he wasn't just seen—he was understood.

Think back to a time when you let your guard down. Maybe you finally said something out loud you'd been holding in. Maybe you told your partner or your brother what you were really carrying.

What happened? Did they judge you—or did they show up for you in a way you didn't expect?

Vulnerability doesn't drive people away. It builds bridges.

ACTION CHALLENGE

Step 1: Voice Your Truth.

Write down one thing you've been afraid to say out loud—a fear, a frustration, an unspoken need.

Then take one step toward vulnerability today:

- Tell someone you trust.
- Record it in a voice memo.
- Even if you don't share it, acknowledge it.

Step 2: Build Real Connection.

Make a list of the three people who matter most to you.

Pick one and reach out today.

- Send a text.
- Make a call.
- Meet up.

Show up as yourself—mask off. Even if it's in a small way.

The walls we build to protect ourselves eventually become the barriers that keep us lonely.

It's time to let someone in, even just a little.

You don't have to bare everything all at once—just enough to remind yourself that real connection starts with truth.

DAY 5

CALL OUT YOUR SHADOWS BEFORE THEY CONTROL YOU

Your past doesn't disappear just because you ignore it. The struggles you don't face don't fade—they tighten their grip.

Think about the weight you've been carrying—regrets, doubts, wounds that still sting when no one's around. How much longer are you going to let them run the show?

Every man carries shadows. Quiet struggles that creep in when the world goes silent. You can try to push them down, drown them out, pretend they don't exist—but they don't go away. They just wait.

What you don't face will keep showing up—again and again—until you do. Your past doesn't own you... unless you refuse to own it first.

I've been there. Trapped by regret. Haunted by mistakes. Held back by the fear of what people would think if they knew the real me. And those shadows? They'll have you feeling stuck—chained to an old version of yourself you swore you'd already outgrown. Like you're walking forward with a rope around your waist, pulling you back to everything you tried to leave behind.

But hear me: those chains aren't unbreakable. The moment you stop running from your past and turn to face it, you take your power back.

You've already proven your strength—you survived it. You made it through. Now it's time to face it, not to relive the pain, but to reclaim your peace.

So today, do something bold. Shine a light on your shadows. Call them out.

Think about how much energy it takes to suppress what you've never dealt with. Now imagine how light you'd feel if you didn't have to carry that weight anymore.

Because once you name it, it stops owning you.

You are not the man you were back then.

You're the man who made it through.

ACTION CHALLENGE

Step 1: Name Your Shadows.

Write down one regret, fear, or unresolved pain you've been avoiding.

Don't hold back—get it out in the open so it loses its grip.

Step 2: Take the First Step.

Choose one small action to start moving forward today:

- Forgive yourself for a mistake you've been holding onto.
- Set a boundary with someone or something that triggers that shadow.
- Have an honest conversation with someone you trust about what's been holding you back.

You've already fought battles that should've taken you out, but you're still here.

That means you have the power to stand up and decide—right now—how the next chapter of your story will be written.

DAY 6

SPEAK UP BEFORE SILENCE DESTROYS YOU

There's a war happening inside you—quiet, invisible, and constant. Doubts. Fears. Worries. All fighting for space in your mind. And every day, you put on the face the world expects. You play the role: be the rock, hold it together, stay strong. But inside? It's chaos. A storm you can't shut off. And the weight of carrying it all by yourself? It's suffocating.

But you don't have to keep living like this.

Real strength isn't pretending everything's fine. It's telling the truth about what's really going on underneath.

I remember nights when I was drowning in my own thoughts—but I couldn't let anyone see it. I thought silence was strength. That keeping it in meant I was in control. But silence didn't protect me—it was pulling me under.

I wasn't just stressed. I was buried.

The day I finally said, "I need help," wasn't the day I fell apart. It was the day I stopped drowning. The moment I spoke up, I felt the shift. Not because everything got easier—but because I wasn't carrying it alone anymore.

Breaking the silence didn't make me weaker. It made me free. It gave me room to breathe, space to heal, and the reminder I needed most:

You don't have to carry this by yourself anymore.

ACTION CHALLENGE

Step 1: Break the Silence.

Write down one thing you've been holding inside—stress, fear, or a burden you've been carrying.

Let it all out, unfiltered.

Step 2: Reach Out.

Take one step toward sharing what you've been holding in.

This could mean:

- Starting a conversation with someone you trust.
- Writing a letter or text to express how you feel.
- Practicing saying "I need to talk" aloud to yourself to make the conversation easier when you're ready.

You weren't meant to go through life alone.

The weight you're carrying might not disappear overnight, but the second you stop holding it alone, it gets lighter.

DAY 7

THE STRENGTH IN SAYING, "THIS IS WHERE I AM"

Acknowledgment is a game changer. It's the moment you stop pretending, look your pain in the eye, and say, "This is where I'm at right now."

That's not weakness. That's power. That's the courage to stop running and start facing what's real.

It's like standing at a crossroads—you can't move forward until you admit where you're standing.

For too long, we've hidden behind masks. Saying "I'm good" when we're barely holding it together. We've been taught to treat acknowledgment like defeat. But here's the truth: it's not facing your reality that breaks you—it's running from it. Every time you bury what you're carrying, it only grows heavier. Denial doesn't protect you—it traps you.

Real strength sounds like this: "I'm not okay, but I'm working on it." That's where transformation begins.

I remember a conversation with a friend who had been pushing himself to the edge—working long hours, handling everything for his family, showing up for everyone but himself. He kept saying, "I'm fine," but you could see it in his eyes—he wasn't.

Then one day, he finally said, "Man, I'm exhausted. I don't know how much longer I can keep this up." That moment didn't make him weak—it made him free. He gave himself permission to be honest. And that honesty gave him a path forward.

Think about a time when you finally faced something head-on. Maybe it was admitting a relationship was draining you. Maybe it was finally telling the truth about your job, your stress, or how much you've been carrying. It probably felt like standing on the edge of a cliff. But once you spoke it out loud, the weight started to lift. You stopped fighting yourself—and started dealing with what's real.

ACTION CHALLENGE

Step 1: Own It.

Take 5 minutes to say out loud, "This is where I am right now," and describe your reality in one sentence.

It doesn't have to be pretty—it just has to be honest.

For example:

"I'm overwhelmed because I've been doing too much for everyone else and not enough for myself."

Hearing your truth spoken aloud can feel freeing.

Step 2: Map the Way Forward.

Write down one specific area where you feel stuck (e.g., work, relationships, health).

Then brainstorm ONE small, actionable step you can take to start moving forward.

For example:

- If your job is draining you, commit to blocking off 15 minutes to look at new opportunities.
- If you've been saying yes to everything, practice saying no to one request this week.

Acknowledgment isn't the end of the story—it's the starting point for change.

You can't rewrite your story if you won't admit where you are.

Own it. Stand in it.

And then start taking the steps to move forward.

Your story isn't finished yet—it's just getting started.

And the man who's willing to say, "This is where I am," is the man who's ready to rise.

DAY 8

TURNING TRIGGERS INTO TOOLS FOR GROWTH

Every man has triggers—those moments when something hits a nerve, and before you can even process it, you're reacting. Snapping. Shutting down. Spinning out. It can happen fast. A tone. A look. A few careless words.

Maybe it's someone dismissing your opinion.

Maybe it's a sharp comment that brings back old feelings of being overlooked.

Maybe it's a small setback that suddenly feels like failure all over again.

These reactions don't come out of nowhere. They're tied to something deeper—wounds you've carried, stories you've believed, or moments that never fully healed. Triggers don't show up just to frustrate you. They show up to show you where the work still is.

And if you don't face them, they'll run the show. You'll keep reacting the same way, feeling like you're stuck in the same cycle—and wondering why.

But what if triggers aren't the enemy? What if they're messengers?

What if every time you get triggered is actually a chance to check in instead of check out?

Your triggers are like road signs. They point to what still needs your attention. They're not there to break you—they're there to teach you.

ACTION CHALLENGE

Step 1: Identify Your Trigger.

Think back to the last time you were triggered.

- What happened?
- What did you feel in that moment? (e.g., "When I wasn't invited to the meeting, I felt overlooked, and it made me angry.")
- What past experience might this be tied to?

Naming the root of the trigger is the first step to managing it.

Step 2: Build Your Trigger Toolkit.

Next time you're triggered, practice this 3-step process:

1. Pause. Take a deep breath and acknowledge the feeling. Don't react—just notice it.

2. Name It. Silently say, "This is my trigger." Remind yourself it's about the past, not the present.

3. Redirect. Choose a different response. Instead of reacting with anger, express yourself calmly or take a step back to process.

FINAL TAKEAWAY

Triggers are teachers.

They're not here to defeat you—they're here to grow you.

And every time you face one with honesty, you take your power back.

Healing doesn't happen by accident—it happens when you stop running from what hurts and start facing it with purpose.

You don't have to keep repeating the same reaction.

You get to choose something different.

One trigger, one choice, one moment at a time—that's how you change your story.

DAY 9

OWN THE MIRROR—THE POWER OF SELF-AWARENESS

If you don't understand yourself, you'll keep repeating the same frustrations, the same failures, the same regrets.

Most men aren't stuck because they lack ability. They're stuck because they never stop to check in. Too busy grinding, pushing, handling what needs to get done—never pausing long enough to ask:

- What's really going on inside me?
- What am I carrying right now?
- What's fueling my reactions, my choices, my mood?

Most men don't ask those questions. And that's exactly why they stay stuck.

ACTION CHALLENGE

Step 1: Take a Self-Awareness Pause.

Find a quiet moment today—no distractions, no excuses.

Close your eyes and ask yourself:

What am I carrying right now?

Don't filter it. Don't analyze. Just let your thoughts surface.

Write down the first three emotions or thoughts that come up, no matter how messy they feel.

Step 2: Reflect and Redirect.

Look at what you wrote down. Next to each one, ask: Where is this coming from?

For example:

- Frustration? Maybe it's because you feel unheard at work.
- Exhaustion? Maybe you've been stretching yourself too thin.
- Resentment? Maybe you've been saying "yes" to everyone but yourself.

Now, next to each one, write one small action you can take to shift it.

- Frustration? Speak up in that next meeting.
- Exhaustion? Set a boundary today.
- Resentment? Do one thing for yourself—without guilt.

Self-awareness isn't about fixing yourself.

It's about finally seeing yourself.

Once you stop reacting on autopilot, you start choosing your next move.

And that's where real power begins.

DAY 10

REDEFINING SUCCESS – WHAT WINNING LOOKS LIKE FOR YOU

If you don't define success for yourself, the world will do it for you. And if you let the world define it, you'll spend your life chasing things that look good on the outside but feel empty when you finally get them.

For too long, men have been told what success should look like:

- Make the money.
- Get the status.
- Stay in control.

Be the provider. Be the strong one. Have the perfect job, the perfect relationship, the perfect life. But how many men check all those boxes—and still feel unfulfilled?

Because none of that matters if it doesn't match what actually makes you feel alive.

I know what that feels like. I remember grinding toward the version of success I thought I was supposed to want:

- Saying yes to things that didn't excite me.
- Taking opportunities because they looked good on paper.
- Measuring myself by someone else's scoreboard.

Until I hit a wall.

I had worked so hard to build something that didn't even feel like mine. That's when I asked myself the question that changed everything:

If I woke up tomorrow with nothing to prove—what kind of life would I actually want?

That one question redefined everything.

I realized success for me wasn't about the numbers or the recognition. It was about freedom:

- Freedom to do meaningful work.
- Freedom to be present with the people I love.
- Freedom to live on my terms.

WHAT ABOUT YOU?

If you weren't chasing approval, what would success look like for you? If you stopped measuring yourself against the world's expectations, what would finally feel right?

Success isn't just about what you accomplish.

It's about how aligned your life feels.

Winning isn't about checking the boxes—it's about building a life that actually belongs to you.

ACTION CHALLENGE

Step 1: Define Your True Success.

Write down the definition of success you've been living by.

Then ask yourself: Does this truly reflect what I value?

If not, rewrite it.

Example:

- ✘ Old definition: Success is making a six-figure income.
- ✔ New definition: Success is having time to be with my family while doing work I'm passionate about.

Step 2: Make a Shift.

Choose ONE thing in your life that doesn't align with your true definition of success.

Take an intentional action today to move closer to your version of winning.

Examples:

- Decline an opportunity that doesn't excite you.
- Block off time for something meaningful—spending time with loved ones or working on a passion project.

Because if you don't take control of your definition of success, someone else will.

And you weren't meant to live a life that doesn't belong to you.

DAY 11

VULNERABILITY IS THE STRENGTH THAT BUILDS CONNECTION

How many times have you swallowed your words, buried your emotions, and told yourself, "I'll handle it alone"? How many moments passed where you wanted to speak up—but stayed silent instead?

From the time we're boys, we're taught to keep it together. Lock it down. Don't let them see you sweat. But ask yourself—what has that silence cost you?

Maybe it was a friendship that faded. A relationship that fell apart. Or years of feeling like no one really knows the real you. Vulnerability isn't weakness—it's the bridge to real connection.

Think about how often you've bottled up your emotions, convinced it was better to carry the weight on your own. Maybe you had a moment where you almost let someone in—but didn't. What did that moment cost you?

Vulnerability isn't about spilling everything to everyone. It's about being real with the people who matter. It's about saying, "This is where I'm at," without fear of being seen differently.

I used to think strength meant carrying everything without complaint. That being silent made me strong. But after carrying too much for too long, I hit a breaking point. And instead of keeping it inside, I told someone I trusted, "I'm not okay."

That moment didn't make me weaker—it set me free. I realized I wasn't alone. That people actually wanted to support me. But I had to give them the chance.

Some of the strongest moments in my life weren't when I held it all together—but when I had the courage to let someone see behind the mask.

ACTION CHALLENGE

Step 1: Name the Emotion.

Write down one struggle or emotion you've been keeping to yourself.

Be specific—don't just say, "I'm stressed."

Dig deeper.

Example: "I'm worried I'm not doing enough for my family."

Step 2: Share with Intention.

Think of someone you trust—a partner, friend, or mentor.

Commit to sharing just one piece of what you wrote with them.

You don't have to over-explain.

Start small:

_"I've been feeling ___, and I need someone to talk to about it."

Watch how opening up lightens the emotional load and creates space for connection.

When you open up, you create space for deeper connections.

You allow others to show up for you and, in turn, inspire them to do the same.

That's how relationships grow.

That's how healing begins.

DAY 12

YOUR CIRCLE DETERMINES YOUR STRENGTH

Look at the three closest people in your life. Are they sharpening you or dulling you? Are they pushing you toward your best self—or keeping you stuck in the same patterns?

They say you're the average of the five people you spend the most time with. So ask yourself: What does your circle say about you?

No man thrives in isolation. But here's the flip side—not everyone around you is good for you. Some people will elevate you, challenge you, and remind you of who you are when you forget. Others will drain you, distract you, or keep you comfortable when you should be growing.

For a long time, I was surrounded—but still felt alone. We laughed. We joked. We talked about everything except what actually mattered. But when life hit me hard? I didn't have anyone I could truly turn to.

I was the one always pouring into everyone else—but no one was pouring into me. And eventually, I felt it. The emptiness. The resentment. The exhaustion of being everyone's lifeline while drowning in silence.

That's when I had to face it: A real circle isn't just about who's around you—it's about who's for you. Not everyone deserves access to your energy. And if you're the only one doing the pouring, it might be time to check who's sitting at your table.

ACTION CHALLENGE

Step 1: Audit Your Circle.

Write down the names of three people you spend the most time with.

Next to each name, ask yourself:

- Do they push me to grow?
- Do they celebrate my wins without jealousy?
- Do they show up for me when life gets heavy?

If the answer is no, consider how you might adjust the energy you give to that relationship.

Step 2: Strengthen Your Bonds.

Reach out to one person who uplifts you and let them know what their support means to you.

Your circle isn't just about who's around you—it's about who's elevating you.

You don't just need company—you need a crew that makes you stronger.

DAY 13

THE STRENGTH IN FACING WHAT YOU FEEL

Some mornings, the weight of the world hits you before you even sit up in bed. And what do most of us do? We slap on a brave face, tell ourselves to tough it out, and keep pushing.

But ask yourself—how often does that actually work? Ignoring what you feel doesn't make it go away. It just drives it deeper. And anything you bury long enough? It finds a way out—usually at the worst possible time.

For the longest time, I told myself I didn't have time to deal with emotions. Stress? Push through. Frustration? Bury it. Anxiety? Ignore it and keep moving. I thought staying focused meant locking my emotions away.

Until one day, it all hit at once. I snapped at someone I loved over something small—not because I was angry with them, but because I'd been carrying too much for too long.

That was the moment it clicked: the more you avoid what you feel, the more power it has over you. Emotions aren't the enemy—they're messengers.

As men, we're taught to treat emotions like liabilities. To hide them. Silence them. Muscle through. But emotions aren't the problem. They're signals. That anger you keep pushing aside? That anxiety sitting in your chest? That low-grade numbness that never really goes away?

They're trying to tell you something.

Ignoring them is like driving with the check engine light on. You might get a few more miles, but eventually—something's going to break down.

ACTION CHALLENGE

Step 1: Check In with Your Body.

Take 5 minutes today to tune into yourself.

Where are you holding tension?

- Jaw?
- Shoulders?
- Chest?
- Stomach?

Then ask yourself: What emotion am I feeling here?

Write down the first word that comes to mind. (Anger? Stress? Sadness?)

Step 2: Release the Weight.

Choose one emotion you identified and take a small action to address it:

- If you're stressed, step away for 10 minutes to breathe or stretch.

- If you're angry, channel it into something physical like a workout.
- If you're sad, reach out to someone who brings you comfort.

This isn't about fixing everything at once.

It's about creating space for your emotions to move through you.

FINAL TAKEAWAY

Emotional awareness isn't weakness—it's wisdom.

Ignoring what you feel doesn't make you stronger—it just makes you a ticking time bomb.

The strongest men aren't the ones who bottle it up. They're the ones who face it, learn from it, and use it.

You either face what you feel—or what you feel will eventually force you to face it.

DAY 14

REWRITING THE STORY YOU TELL YOURSELF

The story you tell yourself about who you are sets the tone for everything—how you move, how you show up, and what you believe is possible. And if that story is filled with doubts, excuses, or "not enoughs," you'll keep shrinking to fit it. But when you rewrite the narrative—when you start seeing yourself as capable and worthy—you stop hesitating and start stepping into the life you were meant to live.

Your self-view shapes your decisions every day. If you believe you're undeserving of good things, you'll downplay your gifts. You'll stay quiet when you should speak up. You'll turn away from opportunities and call it "humility"—when really, it's fear in disguise. But when you start seeing yourself as strong, resilient, and deserving—you move differently. You take risks. You walk with intention. You go after what you want because you know you're worth it.

I've been there—letting doubt set the pace. Telling myself I wasn't ready. Holding back because I thought I had to be perfect before I could show up. But every time I challenged that story—every time I acted despite the fear—I reminded myself of who I really am. And every time I did, I grew stronger.

Your past doesn't define you. You're not the times you fell short—you're the man who got back up. You've already survived what you thought would break you. So why keep living like you're still broken?

It's time to stop magnifying your flaws and start honoring your growth.

> **ACTION CHALLENGE**
>
> **Step 1: Identify the Narrative.**
>
> Write down one limiting belief you've been telling yourself.
>
> (e.g., "I'm not good enough," "I don't deserve success," or "I'll never be able to change.")
>
> **Step 2: Flip the Script.**
>
> Take that belief and rewrite it into a positive affirmation.
>
> Examples:
>
> - ✗ Old belief: "I'm not good enough."
> - ✓ New belief: "I'm growing and capable of more than I realize."
> - ✗ Old belief: "I'll never change."
> - ✓ New belief: "Every small step I take moves me closer to who I want to be."
>
> Read this affirmation out loud three times today.
>
> The words you say to yourself have the power to change how you see your life.

FINAL TAKEAWAY

Seeing yourself clearly isn't arrogance—it's alignment. Because when you finally embrace your worth, you stop waiting for permission. You stop hiding in plain sight. You start moving like a man who belongs in every room he walks into.

It's time to see yourself as the capable, worthy, powerful man you truly are—because that's who you've been all along.

DAY 15

THIS IS WHERE MOST MEN STOP—BUT YOU WON'T

Most men never make it here. They start strong—facing hard truths, breaking cycles, making promises to change—but somewhere along the way, the momentum fades. But you? You're different. You didn't come this far just to stop now.

Self-awareness isn't a one-time thing. It's a process. A daily choice. It's like cleaning a window you didn't realize was dirty. At first, the light feels harsh. It shows you things you weren't ready to see. But the more you stay with it, the clearer everything becomes.

You start to see:

- The cracks that need repairing.
- The burdens you need to let go of.
- The habits that are worth keeping.

ACTION CHALLENGE

Step 1: Commit to One Standard Today.

Instead of writing a list, choose one non-negotiable that you will uphold immediately.

Examples:

- If your standard is "I will not let my phone distract me from family time," turn it off for one hour tonight.
- If your standard is "I will follow through on my word," take care of something you've been procrastinating on today.

Step 2: Proof Over Promises.

Instead of telling someone your non-negotiable, prove it.

Do one thing today that demonstrates your new standard, without explaining it.

FINAL TAKEAWAY

The work you've done so far has been about laying the foundation—brick by brick. But here's what most men don't realize:

A strong foundation means nothing if you don't build on it.

This next phase is where you start doing that.

Not just breaking old patterns, but building something stronger in their place.

Not just healing—but rising.

You're not just becoming aware. You're becoming him.

Are you ready?

Let's build.

PILLAR 2

RESILIENCE IS BUILT, NOT GIVEN

(DAYS 16–29)

By now, you've taken some bold steps. You've faced your struggles, named the weight you've been carrying, and admitted to yourself that things haven't always been okay. That takes courage.

But courage alone isn't enough—you have to build on it.

Naming the pain is just the beginning.

Resilience isn't just about acknowledging the struggle.

It's about rising, adapting, and pressing forward when life pushes you to your limit.

It's not pretending you're fine—it's standing up, even when everything in you wants to stay down.

And let's be clear: you're not born with resilience. You build it.

In the moments when quitting feels easier. In the days when everything says "stop"—but you keep going anyway.

Those weren't lucky breaks.

They were proof of what's already inside you.

But resilience isn't about carrying it all alone.

Too many men are taught that asking for help makes you weak. But that kind of thinking doesn't make you stronger—it just makes the weight heavier.

Real resilience is knowing when to lean in.

When to reach out.

When to let someone help you carry what you were never meant to carry alone.

This phase is about more than just getting through the storm.

It's about learning how to stay steady in it.

Resilience isn't about being unshakable—it's about being adaptable.

It's knowing the wind will blow, and choosing to plant your feet anyway.

In this next stretch, we'll dig into:

- What triggers you—and how to respond without exploding.
- How to feel your emotions without being ruled by them.
- How to create strength that lasts beyond the hard moments.

Yes, vulnerability is coming up again—not because it's trendy, but because it's real.

You don't grow by dodging your emotions. You grow by facing them head-on.

Imagine being the man who doesn't run from discomfort—but leans into it.

Who handles stress without breaking.

Who owns his emotions instead of stuffing them down.

Who gets knocked back—but never off course.

That's the kind of resilience we're building here.

It's not about avoiding hardship.

It's about being equipped to face it—and walk through it with your head up.

The storms won't stop coming. But now, you'll know how to stand in them.

How to bend without breaking.

How to endure without losing yourself.

You've come a long way.

You've faced your past.

You've started building a stronger foundation.

But now? It's time to move from surviving to leading.

This next phase is about ownership.

About stepping into your power.

About shaping life on your own terms—not just reacting to what comes at you.

You're not just learning to stand.

You're learning to lead.

Let's take the next step.

DAY 16

EVERY SETBACK IS A SETUP—IF YOU REFUSE TO STAY DOWN

Life hits hard. It doesn't ask if you're ready. It doesn't care about your plans.

One minute, you think you've got your feet under you—and the next, you're scrambling. Maybe you just lost the job that kept food on the table. Maybe the relationship you thought would last is slipping through your fingers. Maybe the dream you gave everything to just fell apart right in front of you.

And the worst part? The world keeps moving like nothing happened.

I know that feeling. I remember staring at my bank account after losing my job. No backup plan. A new wife. A new house. A new baby. And no idea how I was going to make it. I had two choices: let it break me or get up and fight.

I won't lie—it was scary. There were weeks I barely scraped by. Nights I questioned everything. But somewhere in all of that pressure, I realized something: life doesn't get easier. You just get stronger.

Most men don't quit because they're weak. They quit because they can't see a way forward.

But hear this: a setback doesn't mean you're finished. It means you've been given a choice—to stay down or rise up with something new. When life knocks you flat, it's not the end. It's a chance to rebuild stronger, smarter, and more grounded than before.

ACTION CHALLENGE

Step 1: Rewrite Your Setback.

Write down a specific setback you've faced that felt like the end.

Reflect on what it taught you—what strengths did it reveal, what lessons did you gain, and how did it push you forward?

Step 2: Take the Next Step.

Identify one unresolved challenge lingering from that setback and take action today to address it.

Examples:

- If you're still holding onto regret, write a letter of forgiveness to yourself.

- If you're rebuilding after a loss, take one tangible step toward your goal (update your resume, reach out to a mentor, or set a financial plan).

Setbacks are setups for something greater—but only if you choose to act on them.

DAY 17

CHANGE WILL BREAK YOU OR BUILD YOU—YOU DECIDE

There are moments in life when change doesn't ask for permission—it kicks the door down and flips everything upside down. A job loss. A breakup. A hard truth that the path you're on isn't taking you where you thought it would.

Change can feel like an earthquake, shaking the ground you thought was solid. And in those moments, it's easy to believe change is the enemy. But it's not. Change is what makes you.

I remember thinking change was wrecking me. When I lost my job after a decade of loyalty and consistency, the uncertainty was suffocating. I had a wife, a newborn, and a mortgage—quitting wasn't an option. Everything in me wanted to fight it, to cling to what felt safe. But that change, as painful as it was, forced something greater out of me. It made me bet on myself. It made me dig deeper than I ever had before.

That loss? It wasn't the end. It was the push that moved me into the life I was always meant to build.

Change didn't ruin me. It revealed me.

Change broke my routine—but it built my purpose.

ACTION CHALLENGE

Step 1: Reframe Change.

Think about a recent change that shook you.

Write down what doors it closed, but also what new opportunities it opened.

What possibilities does this change offer that weren't there before?

Step 2: Take a Growth Step.

Pick one uncomfortable but productive action that moves you forward in this change.

Examples:

- If the change left you jobless, commit to reaching out to one connection for support or applying for a position.
- If it's a personal shift, create a small daily habit to ground yourself (a 10-minute reflection, a gratitude practice, or reconnecting with someone who supports you).

Change will shape you, but how it shapes you depends on your response.

You don't control when it happens, but you do control how you respond.

Will you fight it, or will you use it as fuel?

The choice is yours.

DAY 18

CARRY THE WEIGHT OR LET IT CRUSH YOU—THE CHOICE IS YOURS

How often were you told to "man up" as a kid? To bottle up your emotions, tough it out, and never let the cracks show? It's a story most of us have heard—and maybe even lived. But let's call it what it is: That version of toughness doesn't work. It leaves you worn down, disconnected, and carrying more than you were ever meant to bear.

Real strength isn't about shutting down your emotions; it's about standing firm, even when life is coming at you from every angle. We all have those days when it feels like too much. Work deadlines pile up. Family looks to you for answers. The weight of trying to be everything for everyone? It gets heavy.

But strength doesn't come from pretending the load isn't there. It comes from facing it head-on and choosing to show up anyway. That's what resilience really is—not the absence of struggle, but the decision to keep moving through it.

I remember the moment I had to choose between taking a demotion or betting on myself. The fear of letting my family down was overwhelming. But that decision taught me something I'll never forget: Strength isn't about never falling—it's about learning how to get back up, again and again.

Every setback you face shapes you. Into someone stronger. Someone wiser. Someone who refuses to quit.

Your struggles don't define you—your choices do.

ACTION CHALLENGE

Step 1: Lighten the Load.

Write down three things that are currently weighing on you.

For each one, ask yourself:

Is this something I can control, delegate, or let go of?

Step 2: Take One Small Step.

Choose ONE item from your list and act on it:

- If it's work stress, block off 30 minutes to focus on a priority task or set boundaries for the day.

- If it's emotional weight, reach out to someone you trust and share what you're feeling.

- If it's physical exhaustion, give yourself permission to rest or take a walk to recharge.

Real strength isn't about carrying it all—it's about knowing when to share the load or put some of it down.

DAY 19

WIN THE BATTLE IN YOUR MIND BEFORE YOU FIGHT IT IN THE WORLD

Positive thinking isn't about pretending everything's fine. It's not about faking a smile or ignoring what's right in front of you. It's about shifting your focus from what's missing to what's possible. Because how you see your struggle? That's what determines how you move through it.

Most men are taught to brace for impact—to carry the unspoken rules: Provide. Protect. Don't show weakness. So when things don't go as planned, it's easy to spiral. To let fear call the shots. I know that feeling firsthand.

When I left the security of a steady paycheck to build something on my own, the fear was loud. Every time I looked at my family, I questioned if I was making the right move. Doubt kept whispering that I should play it safe—that I was risking too much.

But then I had to ask myself: What if I fail because I believe I will? What if my mindset is the only thing standing between me and what I'm capable of?

ACTION CHALLENGE

Step 1: Create a Gratitude Anchor.

Write down three things you're grateful for right now, but don't stop there.

Choose ONE and turn it into a daily anchor by keeping a physical reminder nearby—

- A photo of loved ones.
- A note to yourself.
- Something symbolic of what you're thankful for.

Place it somewhere you'll see often to remind yourself to focus on what's possible.

Step 2: Mental Reframe Practice.

The next time doubt or fear creeps in, commit to pausing for 30 seconds.

Say out loud:

"What if this works instead of fails?"

Then, write down one action you can take toward a positive outcome, no matter how small.

FINAL TAKEAWAY

Mindset isn't about ignoring the hard stuff—it's about standing in it and deciding how you'll respond. Every time you train your mind to see possibility instead of panic, you're building resilience. You're proving to yourself that even if the odds are stacked, you're built to overcome.

DAY 20

THE STRENGTH TO BE SEEN—WHY HIDING ONLY HURTS YOU

Most men were taught that strength means silence. That the less you show, the stronger you appear. But what if that lie is the very thing breaking you?

Real strength isn't found in pretending—it's in having the courage to be seen, scars and all. The world tells us to be the rock—steady, unshakable, always in control. But let me tell you something: the men who truly inspire aren't the ones who hide their struggles. They're the ones who own them.

"Real strength isn't in how much you can carry—it's in knowing when to be real about the weight."

I used to think strength meant handling everything on my own. I'd be drowning in pressure but still saying, "I got it," even when I didn't. Even when it was breaking me. I convinced myself that asking for help would make me look weak—until my body made the decision for me.

Stress. Exhaustion. I crashed.

And in that moment, I realized: either I start being honest about what I'm carrying, or the weight will bury me.

> **ACTION CHALLENGE**
>
> **Step 1: Own Your Story.**
>
> Take 5 minutes to write down one battle you've faced—a struggle that left a scar but taught you something valuable.
>
> Then, reframe it by writing what that experience taught you about your strength or resilience.
>
> **Step 2: Break the Silence.**
>
> Choose one person in your life whom you trust and share a piece of your story with them.
>
> It doesn't have to be the whole thing—just one moment or lesson you've learned.
>
> Opening up might feel uncomfortable, but it's a step toward connection and healing.

FINAL TAKEAWAY

Hiding doesn't heal. Pretending doesn't make the weight go away—it just makes you feel more alone.

Your scars aren't proof of weakness. They're proof that you made it through. And when you let yourself be seen—not as perfect, but as real—you don't just find freedom. You give the people around you permission to be real, too.

The most dangerous man in the room isn't the one who hides the weight—it's the one who's done hiding.

DAY 21

STOP LETTING DOUBT STEAL FROM YOU

Self-doubt is a thief. It doesn't rob you all at once—it takes you down piece by piece, in whispers that sound like your own voice. It makes you question yourself when you should be standing firm. It tells you you're not ready. Not good enough. Not built for what's in front of you.

But let me tell you something: self-doubt is a liar. It's just noise trying to keep you from stepping into the man you were made to be.

I remember writing my first book—pouring everything I had into it—and then hesitating when it was time to release it. What if people didn't like it? What if no one even cared?

But I pushed through the fear. And that book became a #1 New Release on Amazon.

If I had listened to the doubt, that moment never would've happened. And now, here I am—on my seventh book.

Self-doubt tried to stop me. And I know it's trying to stop you, too.

ACTION CHALLENGE

Step 1: List Three Wins.

Write down three times when you doubted yourself but showed up anyway—and succeeded.

This could be:

- A hard conversation you had.
- A decision to try something new.
- Simply getting through a tough day.

Step 2: Face the Hesitation.

Think about something you've been hesitating on—big or small.

Take one small but deliberate action toward it today.

Examples:

- Send the email or make the call you've been putting off.
- Write down the first step toward a bigger goal you've been procrastinating on.
- Remind yourself: "This doesn't have to be perfect—it just has to start."

FINAL TAKEAWAY

That voice in your head—the one saying you're not ready, not qualified, not enough? It only has power if you believe it. Doubt grows in silence. But it shrinks when you confront it.

You've already proven your strength. You've already made it through things that should've broken you.

Now it's time to prove it to yourself again.

DAY 22

THE MEN WHO STAND WITH YOU DEFINE THE MAN YOU BECOME

No man wins alone. But life will try to convince you otherwise. It'll whisper that strength means carrying it all on your own—that asking for help makes you weak.

But real strength? It's knowing when to lean on your brothers. It's recognizing that the weight gets lighter when it's shared.

Isolation doesn't build warriors—it breaks them.

Think about the times when you felt like you were drowning. When work, family, and the unspoken expectations stacked up like bricks on your chest. Who was there? Who reminded you of your worth when you started to forget?

The men who show up in those moments? That's your crew. That's your foundation.

I remember when I was grinding to build my business from the ground up. I told myself I had to prove I could do it alone. Late nights. Early mornings. Barely getting by. But when I finally let my people in—when I admitted I needed support—it changed everything.

The strong women who raised me, the brothers who wouldn't let me quit—they didn't just hold me up. They pushed me forward.

Sometimes, the difference between breaking and breaking through is the people who refuse to let you fall.

So ask yourself: Who's in your corner? Who calls you higher? Who challenges you, checks you, and makes you better?

And just as importantly—who are you showing up for?

Because relationships aren't one-sided. It's not just about who's there for you. It's about how you pour back into the people who matter.

ACTION CHALLENGE

Step 1: Take Inventory of Your Circle.

Write down the names of the 3-5 people who have been there for you.

Reflect on how they've shown up for you and how they've strengthened you.

Step 2: Strengthen the Bond.

Reach out to one of those people today.

- Send a simple "thank you" text.
- Make a call to check in.
- Schedule time to reconnect.

FINAL TAKEAWAY

Your crew is your armor. The people you surround yourself with will either sharpen you or dull your edge.

Choose wisely.

And once you know who's really in your corner—let them know you see them.

Send that text. Make that call.

Because no man stands strong alone.

And no man rises without someone in his corner.

DAY 23

THE STRENGTH TO LET SOMEONE IN

Men are masters of locking things away. From the time we're boys, we're taught to toughen up, swallow our emotions, and "figure it out" on our own. It's what the world expects, right? But that expectation? It's a slow poison. The more we suppress, the more we isolate. And the more we isolate, the more we convince ourselves that nobody would understand us anyway.

Let me ask you something—when was the last time you really let someone in? Not surface talk. Not playing it cool. I mean the kind of honesty where you admit that you're struggling. That you don't have it all figured out. That the weight you carry is heavier than you let on.

I used to think keeping it all inside was control. That silence meant strength. That if I didn't talk about it, the pressure would eventually fade. But that's not how it works. What we bury doesn't disappear— it multiplies. It turns into stress, anxiety, anger… and eventually, numbness.

The moment I started letting people in, everything shifted. I wasn't just venting—I was giving myself permission to be human. And in return, I gained what I didn't even know I was missing: real connection. Real brotherhood. Real strength.

ACTION CHALLENGE

Step 1: Open the Door.

Think of one person you trust but haven't fully opened up to.

Take a small step today:

- Start with one sentence like, "I've been carrying a lot lately."
- Let them know you're working on sharing more and invite them into your process.

Step 2: Practice Vulnerability with Yourself.

Write down what you've been carrying—stress, fear, or something unresolved.

Read it out loud to yourself as practice before sharing it with someone else.

FINAL TAKEAWAY

The people who matter want to know the real you.

They want to show up for you.

But they can't—if you never open the door.

DAY 24

THE FREEDOM YOU'VE BEEN SEARCHING FOR IS IN YOUR TRUTH

How many times have you swallowed your words, nodded when you wanted to push back, or smiled when you felt like screaming? How often have you let silence speak for you—just because speaking up felt like a risk?

Whether it's at work, in your relationships, or even with yourself, there's this constant pressure to keep it all together. To be solid. To be unshaken.

But let's be real—holding everything in doesn't make you stronger. It just makes the cracks run deeper.

WHAT HAPPENS WHEN YOU STOP HIDING?

We tell ourselves we're protecting something by keeping certain parts of us hidden. But what we're really doing is building walls that keep people out—and trap us in.

We think if we just keep pushing, keep pretending, keep the mask on a little longer… maybe one day we'll finally feel as put together as we look. But deep down, you already know that day never comes.

So, what would happen if you let someone see the real you?

Not the polished version.

Not the one that's learned how to play it cool.

But the version that's tired of carrying the weight alone.

That kind of honesty doesn't make you weak. It makes you free.

Every time you choose to be real, you loosen the grip of everything that's been holding you back.

ACTION CHALLENGE

Step 1: Unmask Yourself.

Write down one truth about yourself that you've been hesitant to admit, even to yourself.

It could be a fear, a regret, or something you've been holding back.

Acknowledge it without judgment.

Step 2: Share Your Truth.

Choose one person you trust and share a piece of that truth with them.

This could be as simple as saying:

- "I've been struggling with this."
- "I need to let this out."

Start with someone who has proven they can hold space for you.

FINAL TAKEAWAY

Freedom begins when you stop hiding from yourself and let others see the real you. Take off the mask. Be real. And watch how it transforms not just your world—but the worlds of everyone around you.

DAY 25

PERFECTION IS A PRISON—BREAK FREE AND LIVE

Chasing perfection is like running on a treadmill—you're putting in the effort, but you're not getting anywhere. No matter how much you accomplish, that voice in your head still whispers, "It's not enough." The pressure to be flawless isn't making you better—it's keeping you stuck.

We convince ourselves that if we could just get everything right, we'd finally feel worthy. But perfection isn't a standard—it's a cage. It keeps you second-guessing. Overthinking. Waiting for the "perfect" moment that never comes.

THE COST OF PERFECTIONISM

Think about the times you felt like you had to nail everything. At work—trying to meet every demand without slipping up. At home—telling yourself that if you weren't the "perfect" father, husband, or son, you were falling short.

That voice in your head? The one saying anything less than perfect isn't good enough? That's not discipline. That's self-sabotage.

Failure isn't the enemy. The real enemy is the fear that keeps you from even starting.

Perfection isn't a goal—it's an excuse dressed up like one. It stops you from making moves. Every mistake, every misstep, every stumble—they don't mean you're failing. They mean you're in the game.

The real failure? Letting fear of imperfection keep you from showing up at all.

ACTION CHALLENGE

Step 1: Call Out Perfectionism.

Write down one area in your life where perfectionism has been holding you back.

Next to it, list one thing you've avoided or procrastinated on because you're afraid of not doing it perfectly.

Step 2: Take an Imperfect Step.

Do the thing you've been avoiding—but let it be messy.

- Write the email without over-editing.
- Have the tough conversation without rehearsing every word.
- Tackle the project knowing it won't be flawless—but it will be done.

Progress beats perfection. Every time.

FINAL TAKEAWAY

Letting go of perfection isn't lowering your standards—it's freeing yourself from the ones that never really mattered. Imagine what your life would feel like if you weren't constantly chasing an impossible ideal. Imagine moving without anxiety. Showing up without the pressure to perform.

You are enough.

Not when you hit every mark.

Not when you prove yourself again.

Right now.

Your life isn't waiting on perfection.

It's waiting on you.

Take the step.

DAY 26

THE FREEDOM IN OWNING WHAT YOU FEEL

When was the last time you actually sat with what you were feeling? Not shoved it down. Not drowned it in work, a drink, or a scroll through your phone. But really sat with it—named it, owned it, let yourself process it?

Most of us were taught to move through life like warriors—head down, chest out, emotions locked behind the armor. But that armor doesn't protect you. It traps you. And the longer you avoid what you're feeling, the heavier it gets.

Here's something most men won't say out loud: If you don't deal with it, it will deal with you.

Either you acknowledge the weight—or one day, your body, your relationships, or your peace of mind will make the decision for you.

I used to pride myself on how much I could carry without breaking. But breaking doesn't always look like snapping.

It looks like shutting down.

It looks like snapping over nothing.

It looks like feeling disconnected, even when you're surrounded by people who love you.

I had to learn the hard way: feeling something doesn't make you weak.

Owning it doesn't make you soft—it makes you free.

ACTION CHALLENGE

Step 1: Name the Emotion.

Sit in a quiet space for 5 minutes and ask yourself:

"What am I really feeling right now?"

Write down the first word or phrase that comes to mind—anger, frustration, sadness, or even joy.

Don't overthink it—just name it.

Step 2: Release the Emotion.

Choose a healthy way to process what you're feeling:

- Go for a walk or workout to release tension.
- Write a letter (you don't have to send it) to someone tied to that emotion.
- Talk it out with someone who will listen without judgment.

FINAL TAKEAWAY

Your emotions aren't your enemy—they're your guide.

Keep ignoring them, and you'll keep losing your way.

But own what you feel?

You'll start finding yourself again.

Because a man who understands himself is a man who can change his life.

DAY 27

REAL STRENGTH IS KNOWING WHEN TO REACH OUT

Let's talk about asking for help. For so many of us, it feels like admitting defeat. We've been conditioned to believe that needing support means we're weak. But that's a lie. The strongest men aren't the ones who suffer in silence—they're the ones who know when to lean on others.

Strength isn't about doing it all alone. It's about building a life where people walk beside you—especially when the road gets rough. Think back to a time when life felt overwhelming. Did you put up walls, convinced you had to figure it out by yourself?

I've been there. I remember the early days of building my business. The pressure was relentless. I thought asking for help would make me look like I didn't have it together. So I struggled in silence, trying to carry it all on my own.

But I was wrong.

When I finally opened up to my crew—my mentors, friends, and family—I realized something powerful: asking for help wasn't weakness. It was wisdom. It wasn't a step backward. It was the reason I could keep moving forward.

ACTION CHALLENGE

Step 1: Create Your Support Crew.

Write down the names of three people in your life whom you trust to support you when things get heavy.

Reach out to at least one of them today—whether it's a text, a call, or setting up a time to talk.

Start small, even if it's just to check in.

Step 2: Break the Silence.

The next time you feel overwhelmed, practice saying, "I need help."

You don't have to dive into everything at once, but let someone know what you're facing.

Start by sharing one specific thing on your mind.

FINAL TAKEAWAY

When you open up and ask for help, you're not just lifting the weight off your shoulders—you're giving people a chance to stand with you. Real connection is built in the moments when you allow yourself to be seen—not just as strong, but as human.

Vulnerability isn't a weakness—it's an invitation.

And the strongest men? They're the ones who have the courage to say:

"I don't have to do this alone."

DAY 28

THE BRIDGES BUILT BY OPENING UP

How many times have you wanted to say something real—but stopped yourself? How many moments have passed where you could've spoken up, but you swallowed the words instead? Maybe it was because you thought no one would understand. Maybe it was the fear of being judged. Or maybe you just convinced yourself, "I'll deal with it on my own."

But here's the thing—every time you lock people out, you're not protecting yourself. You're building a wall that keeps you lonely.

Real connection isn't built on perfection. It's built on truth. And no man was meant to carry everything alone.

For most of my life, I kept things to myself. Not because I didn't trust people, but because that's what I was used to. I carried the stress, the doubts, the silent battles—telling myself, "I got it." Until one day, I didn't.

I remember sitting with someone I trusted, the weight of everything pressing on me. They asked how I was doing, and for the first time, I didn't brush it off. I didn't downplay it. I just told the truth.

And instead of being judged, I was understood. Instead of feeling weak, I felt lighter.

That moment shifted something in me. Because I realized I had spent years carrying things I never had to carry alone.

ACTION CHALLENGE

Step 1: Share One Real Thing.

Choose one person you trust and share something meaningful that's been on your heart.

It doesn't have to be monumental—just something real.

If speaking it feels overwhelming, write it out first.

Then, share it in person, via text, or email.

Step 2: Build the Habit.

Schedule one intentional check-in every week—with a friend, family member, or mentor.

Use this time to be honest about what's going on in your life and to hear them out as well.

Connection grows with consistency.

FINAL TAKEAWAY

Opening up is a muscle. The more you use it, the stronger it gets. Every time you choose honesty, you take weight off your shoulders—and off someone else's too. The weight of the world isn't meant for one man to carry.

The strongest bridges aren't built on perfection—they're built on trust. And you build that trust one real conversation at a time.

DAY 29

MASTERING EMOTIONAL DISCIPLINE

Emotions are powerful. They can fuel your drive, deepen your relationships, and push you toward growth. But if you're not careful, they can also control your reactions, cloud your judgment, and lead to choices you regret.

Emotional discipline isn't about suppressing what you feel. It's about understanding your emotions, channeling them, and responding with intention.

Think about the last time your emotions got the best of you. Maybe it was:

- Frustration at work that made you say something you didn't mean.
- An argument at home where emotions took over instead of solutions.
- Doubt or insecurity that kept you stuck overthinking, afraid to move.

Those moments don't define you. But they do show you where the work is.

Emotional discipline is the ability to pause, process, and choose your next move—instead of letting your emotions choose for you.

I've had moments where I let anger or fear take the wheel. I reacted, then looked back and realized how much power I gave away. That's when I learned: emotional discipline isn't about being cold or detached. It's about feeling fully—and still responding wisely. It's about owning your emotions before they own you.

ACTION CHALLENGE

Step 1: Identify Your Emotional Default.

What's the one emotion that tends to take over—anger, frustration, impatience?

Write down a recent situation where it controlled your response.

Step 2: Break the Pattern.

The next time you feel that emotion rising, do one thing differently:

- If you usually react with anger, commit to walking away for one minute before responding.
- If frustration shuts you down, challenge yourself to express how you feel in a calm sentence.
- If impatience makes you snap, commit to slowing your breathing before you speak.

Your emotions don't control you.

You control them.

Prove it.

FINAL TAKEAWAY

Emotional discipline isn't built in a day. It's built in the quiet, ordinary moments when you:

- Choose to pause instead of react.
- Breathe instead of snap.
- Lead instead of lose it.

You'll be tested. But every time you choose intention over impulse, you take back power.

Master this—and you don't just show up calm.

You show up dangerous in the right way—steady, grounded, and fully in control of the man you're becoming.

THE MAN YOU'RE CALLED TO BE

PILLAR 3

STEP INTO THE MAN YOU WERE BUILT TO BE

(DAYS 30–45)

Resilience kept you standing. Now it's time to start moving.

So far, we've been laying the foundation—facing hard truths, rebuilding your strength, and shifting the way you see yourself. But at some point, you've got to stop thinking about who you could be and start stepping into who you already are.

This is where surviving ends—and leading begins.

Power isn't about control, intimidation, or trying to impress people. Real power is alignment. It's knowing who you are, standing on what you believe, and moving with intention and conviction—whether people get it or not.

It's about leading from a place of clarity and courage, not fear or doubt. And it's about choosing—every single day—to show up as your full, authentic self. Not as the man the world expects. Not as the man you've been pretending to be. But as the man you truly are.

You weren't made to live life on autopilot, waiting for something to happen. You were built to build. To lead. To pour into others. To leave your mark. But stepping into that kind of power? It takes work.

It means:

- Challenging the voices that tell you you're not enough.
- Dropping the baggage that's been keeping you small.
- Facing the discomfort that comes with showing up boldly and consistently.

In this phase, you'll learn what it really means to own your power. You'll start to:

- Recognize and use your strengths.

- Push through fear instead of waiting to feel ready.
- Take intentional, measurable steps toward the life you want.

You'll let go of patterns that kept you stuck—and start building habits that raise your standards.

Every step forward will bring you closer to the man you're becoming. A man who doesn't need to perform confidence, because he's rooted in it. A man who leads with humility, focus, and purpose.

But this isn't just about your growth. This is about who you become for the people around you.

Because when you rise, it doesn't stop with you. Your courage gives others permission to grow. Your decision to stop shrinking sets a new standard for what strength really looks like.

So ask yourself—what would shift if you stopped playing small? What would change if you showed up like the man you already know you're capable of being?

That's the impact you were built for. Not just in your own life—but in the lives of those who look to you for strength.

But hear this: power without stability is fragile. If you don't know who you are, life will keep pulling you off course. Every storm. Every setback. Every opinion.

That's what this next phase is about—learning how to hold your ground. To stay centered in who you are. To walk through fire without losing yourself.

Because real power isn't about what you achieve. It's about who you remain when everything around you gets tested.

DAY 30

SHUTTING DOWN THE VOICE THAT HOLDS YOU BACK

There's a voice in your head that never shuts up. It waits for quiet moments to creep in and whisper, "You're not doing enough." Or worse—"You'll never be enough."

That voice? It's not your truth. It's fear, trying to take the wheel. And just because it's loud doesn't mean it's right.

THE VOICE EVERY MAN BATTLES

Every man has faced that inner critic—the one that magnifies your mistakes, replays your failures on a loop, and tries to convince you that who you were at your lowest is all you'll ever be.

But hear me: that voice is not you. The men you look up to—the ones who walk with confidence and calm? They've battled that same voice. They just refused to let it win.

They remind themselves—over and over—that strength isn't found in perfection. It's found in the comeback. In every time they got back up, learned the lesson, and moved forward anyway.

ACTION CHALLENGE

Step 1: Fact-Check Your Doubts.

Write down three negative thoughts you've been wrestling with

Then, for each one, write down specific evidence that proves it wrong.

Examples:

- Doubt: "I always mess things up."
- Truth: "I've faced tough situations before and figured them out."
- Doubt: "I'll never be successful."
- Truth: "I've already overcome challenges that prove I can keep growing."

Step 2: Change the Script.

Choose one of those doubts and rewrite it as a positive affirmation.

Example:

✘ "I'm not good enough."

✔ "I've overcome challenges before, and I'm capable of doing it again."

Keep that affirmation somewhere visible to remind yourself daily.

FINAL TAKEAWAY

Your worth isn't found in checked boxes or flawless performance. It's in how you keep showing up. How you keep growing. How you keep going.

That voice will always try to pull you back into self-doubt. But you get to decide what you believe.

So, remind yourself of this: You weren't put here to be perfect.

You were put here to be real.

And that is more than enough.

DAY 31

YOU BELONG—WALK IN IT

Have you ever walked into a room and felt like you didn't belong? Like everyone else had it figured out and you were just trying to keep up?

That's imposter syndrome—and it's a battle more men face than we admit. No matter how much we've achieved, there's often that quiet voice saying, "You don't deserve to be here."

But let's be clear: you didn't just end up here by accident. You earned this. Every late night. Every sacrifice. Every moment you pushed through when quitting would've been easier. That wasn't luck. That was you. That was grit. That was strength. And that's why you're standing here now.

The doubt you feel? It's not weakness—it's proof that you care. But caring doesn't mean you're not ready. It means what you're doing matters.

What most men don't realize is this: when you carry yourself like you belong, you don't just shift your own mindset—you shift the atmosphere. You give other men permission to do the same. Because confidence isn't just about how you feel—it's about the example you set.

Too many men shrink. Play small. Wait for someone to validate their place. But when you do that, who loses? Your sons? Your brothers? The men watching you to see what's possible?

ACTION CHALLENGE

Step 1: Write Your Story.

Take 10 minutes to write down your journey—the challenges, victories, and lessons learned.

Focus on the grit and perseverance that got you where you are today.

This is your proof that you've earned your place.

Step 2: Step Into Your Power.

Choose one action today that reinforces your belonging.

Examples:

- Speak up in a meeting.
- Take the lead on a project.
- Simply stand tall and walk into a space with confidence.

FINAL TAKEAWAY

Imposter syndrome isn't a sign you're not qualified—it's proof you're standing in new territory. Instead of shrinking back, take it as a signal: it's time to rise.

You don't need to fake it. Just walk in it.

You've already earned your place. Now own it—fully.

DAY 32

BREAKING GENERATIONAL CYCLES

Every man carries a legacy. Some of it is filled with pride, strength, and wisdom. But some of it runs deep with pain, silence, and unspoken struggles we were never taught to name.

Maybe you were taught to never cry. To stay quiet. To believe that providing was the only way to prove you loved someone. But understand this: You don't have to carry those beliefs forward.

Breaking generational cycles isn't just an act of rebellion—it's an act of leadership.

It's saying:

I won't pass down what broke me.

I'll raise my sons to speak and feel.

I'll build relationships rooted in truth—not just survival.

Because you're not just healing for yourself—you're healing for every man who comes after you.

ACTION CHALLENGE

Step 1: Own Your Story.

Write down one lesson you learned growing up that no longer serves you.

Example:

"I was taught that real men don't ask for help, but I'm learning that strength is in community."

Step 2: Make a New Rule.

Decide one new standard you will live by and pass down.

Examples:

- "In my house, men talk about how they feel."
- "I will teach my children that their worth isn't tied to how much they produce."

FINAL TAKEAWAY

Confidence isn't just for you—it's for the men coming after you. Breaking cycles isn't about blaming the past. It's about choosing something better. The world doesn't need more men repeating the patterns. It needs more men rewriting them.

The only question left is—will you be the one to change the story?

DAY 33

THE WINS THAT PROVE YOU'RE BECOMING HIM

As men, we're wired to push forward—to chase the next goal, the next challenge, the next level. But in the grind, we often overlook the small wins that prove we're growing. The moments we showed up even when it was hard. The decisions we made that reflected not just who we were—but who we're becoming.

WHEN WAS THE LAST TIME YOU GAVE YOURSELF CREDIT?

Not just for the big victories, but for the quiet ones: choosing patience instead of frustration. Speaking up when it would've been easier to stay silent. Showing up when walking away would've been easier.

These aren't just moments—they're evidence. Bricks in the foundation of the man you're building. Proof that growth is happening, even when it doesn't feel loud.

ACTION CHALLENGE

Step 1: Celebrate Your Wins.

Write down three wins from the past week—big or small—that show how you're growing.

For example:

- Choosing patience when you wanted to react.
- Staying consistent with a goal.
- Showing kindness when it was easier not to.

Step 2: Honor a Win Publicly.

Share one of those wins with someone you trust—a friend, partner, or mentor.

Let them celebrate with you and affirm your growth.

FINAL TAKEAWAY

The man you're becoming isn't built in a single leap—it's built in the small, quiet choices you make when no one's watching. Success isn't just milestones or recognition. It's how you show up when it's hard. How you keep moving when no one's clapping.

The world will always try to rush you to what's next. But today? Slow down. Look around. Give yourself credit.

You're not who you were—and that's the win.

DAY 34

WHEN EGO KEEPS YOU STUCK

Sometimes, the biggest thing in your way isn't the world around you—it's the man in the mirror. Ego sneaks in, making you feel like you've got something to prove. Even when you're carrying battles no one else can see, ego will have you acting like everything's fine. Holding onto it might feel like strength—but most times, it's what's keeping you stuck.

THE COST OF EGO

Think about the times you stayed silent when you should've asked for help. Not because you didn't need it—but because you didn't want to look weak. Or the moments when pride kept you from admitting you were wrong. Even when it could've saved a relationship. Even when it could've brought healing.

That's not power. That's a prison.

Now imagine dropping the ego. Owning your mistakes instead of hiding from them. Asking for help without shame. Leading from a place of humility, not pride.

That's not weakness—it's wisdom. The strongest men aren't the ones who act like they've got it all figured out. They're the ones willing to grow, to learn, and to change.

ACTION CHALLENGE

Step 1: Reflect on Ego's Cost.

Write down one moment when your pride held you back or cost you something valuable.

What would have changed if you had let humility lead?

Step 2: Practice Humility Today.

Take one action today to lead with humility.

This could mean:

- Apologizing for a mistake.
- Asking for help.
- Genuinely listening without the need to respond.

FINAL TAKEAWAY

Humility doesn't shrink you—it expands you. It deepens relationships, builds trust, and opens doors that pride would've slammed shut.

So today, choose one small act of humility. Say the apology. Admit what you don't know. Let someone else be heard. That choice won't make you less of a man.

It'll make you a better one.

DAY 35
BUILD THE BELIEF THAT BUILDS YOU

Believing in yourself isn't arrogance. It's not about pretending you've got it all figured out. It's about trusting that no matter what life throws your way—you can face it, handle it, and come out stronger.

But that kind of belief doesn't just show up one day. It's a muscle. One that grows with every decision you make, every small win you claim, every time you keep going when doubt tries to shut you down.

YOUR WORTH ISN'T IN WHAT THE WORLD SAYS— IT'S IN WHO YOU ARE

In a world that measures men by their income, their job title, or the car they drive, it's easy to feel like you're not measuring up. But your worth? It's in your resilience. It's in how you show up when no one's watching. It's in the way you refuse to let setbacks define you.

When you truly start believing in yourself, you stop chasing validation—and start living on your own terms.

YOU'VE ALREADY PROVEN MORE THAN YOU GIVE YOURSELF CREDIT FOR.

Think about it: the tough decisions you've made. The times you stood up for yourself when it would've been easier to stay quiet. The nights you kept pushing when quitting seemed like the only option. Those moments weren't just survival—they were proof.

Proof that you're capable.

Proof that you're resilient.

Proof that you're ready for more.

ACTION CHALLENGE

Step 1: Declare Your Goal.

Write down one bold goal you've been holding back on.

Say it out loud and commit to taking one small step toward it today—whether it's researching, planning, or starting.

Step 2: Create a Proof List.

Write down three times you've overcome challenges or doubts in the past.

Keep this list where you can see it as a reminder of your strength and capability.

FINAL TAKEAWAY

Now imagine what your life could look like if you moved like you believed it. What would you chase? What limits would you break?

You don't need anyone else's permission to go after what you want. You just need your own.

So today, take the step. Not for them—for you.

Prove to yourself that you're the man for the job.

DAY 36

LIVE YOUR LEGACY NOW

Every man carries weight—the pressure to provide, to protect, to perform. But legacy isn't something you leave behind someday. Legacy is how you live today.

It's in the decisions you make when no one's watching. It's in the values you pass down, the standards you uphold, the way you show up when it's hard. You're not just writing your story—you're shaping someone else's. Right now.

Every move you make lays a brick. Every word you speak sets a tone. Legacy doesn't wait. It's built in real time.

THE WEIGHT OF INFLUENCE

Think about the men who shaped you. Some taught you strength, patience, or integrity. Others? They showed you exactly what not to be. Either way, they left an imprint. And now—it's your turn.

You've got the power to carry forward the best of what you learned... and to break the cycles that held your people back. That's not easy. But neither is living with regret.

Growth over comfort. Truth over denial.

That's how you build something that outlives you. Not just success. Significance.

ACTION CHALLENGE

Step 1: Define Your Legacy.

Write down three core values that define the man you want to be.

(Examples: Integrity, Kindness, Resilience.)

Step 2: Live It Out.

For each value, choose one tangible action to express it today:

- Integrity: Have an honest conversation you've been avoiding.

- Kindness: Reach out to someone you've lost touch with and let them know you appreciate them.

- Resilience: Commit to finishing a task you've been procrastinating on.

FINAL TAKEAWAY

Legacy isn't later—it's now.

It's not about waiting for the right moment.

It's about being the man you want to be remembered for—right now.

DAY 37

OWNING YOUR TRUTH & STANDING FIRM IN RELATIONSHIPS

Relationships come with expectations—some loud, some silent. The pressure to settle down, move at someone else's pace, or fit into a version of yourself that isn't real can make you question what you actually want.

But before you can build a relationship that's real, you've got to get brutally honest with yourself. What are you ready for? What do you value? What do you want your relationship to feel like—not just look like?

Owning your truth doesn't start with telling somebody else. It starts with telling yourself.

THE POWER OF CLARITY

Think about your past relationships. Were you all in—or just going through the motions? Did you say yes when you wanted to say no? Did you stay quiet just to keep the peace?

That doesn't make you weak. It makes you human. But those moments can become your mirror. Growth happens when you stop running from those reflections and start making intentional choices.

Clarity is power. It gives you the strength to communicate what you need without guilt. To set boundaries and actually honor them. To stop bending who you are just to be chosen.

If you're looking for commitment, say that. If you're not ready, say that too. But whatever you do—don't lie to yourself just to keep someone else comfortable.

ACTION CHALLENGE

Step 1: Learn from the Past.

Reflect on your past relationships and write down one key lesson you've learned about what you truly need or want in a partner.

Step 2: Align Your Actions with Your Truth.

Identify one boundary or truth you haven't been honest about (with yourself or someone else).

Take one small step today to align your actions with that truth—whether that's:

- Setting a boundary.
- Having a conversation.
- Deciding to let go of something that doesn't fit.

FINAL TAKEAWAY

Owning your truth is where real love starts. Not in performance. Not in pressure. But in presence. You don't need to become someone else to be loved. You need to be you—fully, honestly, and without apology.

DAY 38

STOP WASTING TIME ON THE WRONG PEOPLE

Few things cut deeper than wasted time—especially when you gave it everything.

You don't get back the years you spent trying to make something work that was never right for you. And too often, men stay in relationships that drain them—not because they're happy, but because it's familiar.

A relationship that doesn't align with who you are or what you need will never become what you hope it could be. No amount of effort, loyalty, or patience can fix a connection that's fundamentally off.

THE TRUTH ABOUT THE RIGHT PERSON

The right person won't make you:

- Constantly prove your worth.
- Beg for respect, consistency, or peace.
- Silence your needs to avoid conflict.
- Lose yourself just to keep them.

You don't owe anyone unlimited chances. Staying in something that's not working just because you've already invested time doesn't make it worth more. That's not commitment—it's self-betrayal.

The moment you realize a relationship is taking more from you than it's giving, you owe it to yourself to be honest about whether it's still worth it.

ACTION CHALLENGE

Step 1: Own Your Past Choices.

Write down one relationship or connection (past or present) that drained you more than it fulfilled you.

Ask yourself:

- What signs did I overlook?
- What did it cost me?

Step 2: Set a New Standard.

Write down one clear, non-negotiable value or boundary you'll uphold in future relationships.

Examples:

- "I won't settle for a relationship where I feel unheard."
- "I won't stay in a connection where I'm constantly proving my worth."

FINAL TAKEAWAY

Your time, your peace, and your energy are sacred. Don't spend them proving your worth to someone who can't see it.

DAY 39

BRIDGING THE GAP

Relationships are like bridges—they connect us to the people who matter most. But over time, life has a way of wearing those bridges down. The stress of work. Misunderstandings left unresolved. Expectations never voiced. Little by little, the cracks form.

Maybe you've felt it—the silence that lingers too long. The tension that hangs in the air. The wall that showed up before you even realized it was being built.

DISTANCE DOESN'T HAPPEN OVERNIGHT

It creeps in through unsaid words, missed opportunities, and choosing comfort over conversation. But the strength of a relationship isn't found in how well you avoid conflict—it's in how committed you are to rebuilding after it breaks.

Bridges don't fix themselves. Reconnection takes effort. Vulnerability. The willingness to meet in the middle—even when it would be easier to shut down and walk away.

Think about a relationship in your life that feels strained. Maybe it's a friend you've grown apart from. A partner you've been clashing with. A family member whose absence feels like a weight that never quite lifts.

What would it take to start closing that gap? Sometimes it's a text. A call. A small gesture that says, "You matter." Other times, it's a real conversation—one where you both put down your defenses and actually listen. Not to argue. Not to win. But to understand.

ACTION CHALLENGE

Step 1: Reflect and Reach Out.

Think of one relationship that feels distant.

Write down one specific reason why the gap might have formed (e.g., lack of communication, a misunderstanding, or simply time and distance).

Then, take a small step to reconnect today:

- Send a text saying, "Hey, I've been thinking about you. Let's catch up soon."
- Schedule a call or set a time to meet in person.

Step 2: Initiate a Bridge Moment.

Choose one way to show vulnerability and rebuild trust:

- Share a memory or something meaningful about the relationship that you value.
- Start a conversation with, "I miss how things used to be, and I'd like to reconnect. What can we do to start fresh?"

FINAL TAKEAWAY

Rebuilding relationships isn't about grand gestures—it's about small, consistent acts that send a message: I still care. I'm still here. Let's find our way back.

DAY 40

BREAKING THE SILENCE—CREATING SPACES FOR REAL CONNECTION

How often do you feel something weighing on you, but you keep it in—because you don't know how to say it, or you're not sure anyone would even listen?

For a lot of men, opening up feels like stepping into unfamiliar territory. Maybe you were taught to lock your emotions away. Maybe you're afraid that if you speak up, you'll be judged… or worse—ignored.

So you stay silent. You put on the face that says, "I got it handled."

But here's what they don't tell you: Silence doesn't heal—it isolates.

THE POWER OF CREATING SAFE SPACES

Imagine what it would feel like to have a space where you could be real—where trust replaces judgment.

Picture sitting with your partner, your best friend, or even your child, knowing you can share your struggles, fears, and hopes—without shame. Without hesitation. Without needing to play a role.

That kind of connection doesn't just show up—it's built.

One honest moment at a time.

One conversation at a time.

One choice to be real, even when it's uncomfortable.

ACTION CHALLENGE

Step 1: Share One Real Thing.

Identify one thing you've been keeping to yourself—something you've wanted to share but haven't.

It could be a worry, a goal, or even just how you've been feeling.

Choose someone you trust and start the conversation with:

"Can I talk to you about something I've been holding in?"

Step 2: Create a Safe Space for Others.

Be the one to initiate a moment of real connection.

- Reach out to a friend, partner, or family member and ask, "How are you, really?"
- Practice listening without judgment, creating an environment where they feel safe to open up, too.

FINAL TAKEAWAY

Breaking the silence starts with one honest moment. And then another.

Build the habit of real conversation—one step at a time.

Being open doesn't make you weak. It makes you real. And real is where connection lives.

Let the people in your life see you—not just what you do, but who you are underneath it all.

That's where real relationships grow. That's where freedom begins.

DAY 41

STRENGTH IN LEANING ON EACH OTHER

Life can feel like a fight—like you're in the ring, taking hits from every direction. Work. Family stress. Your own thoughts. And sometimes, it feels like you're swinging alone, trying to prove you can handle it all.

But strength isn't about going solo. It's about knowing when to reach for the hand that's reaching for you.

THE TRUTH ABOUT CONNECTION

Think about the relationships that matter most—your partner, your friends, your family. How often do you really let them in?

It's easy to convince yourself you're protecting them by staying quiet. But the truth is, they want to be there for you. Connection isn't a weakness—it's a lifeline. You don't lose strength by leaning on someone. You gain it.

The strongest men aren't the ones who carry everything on their own. They're the ones who build a circle strong enough to share the weight.

ACTION CHALLENGE

Step 1: Build Your Circle.

Identify two people you trust who have been there for you in the past.

Reach out to one of them today—

- Send a text.
- Make a call.
- Plan a quick coffee chat.

Share something you've been dealing with, no matter how small, and ask how they're doing in return.

Step 2: Be the Support.

Flip the focus.

Think of one person in your life who might be carrying a lot right now.

Check in with them and ask:

"How can I support you today?"

Offering support builds bonds that are mutually uplifting.

FINAL TAKEAWAY

Real strength is found in the connections we keep—and the ones we let keep us.

You don't have to carry this alone.

Together, we hold each other up.

Together, we move forward.

Together, we rise.

DAY 42

THE KIND OF MAN WHO TRULY SEES PEOPLE

Life moves fast. You're handling responsibilities, pushing through challenges, and carrying weight most people don't even notice.

But here's something to sit with—every person you cross paths with is carrying something too. Just like you, they're hoping to feel understood. Not just for what they do, but for who they are.

THE SUPERPOWER OF EMPATHY

Empathy isn't just a nice trait—it's a superpower. It's what separates surface-level interactions from real connection.

Think about the last time someone really listened to you. No interruptions. No nodding while waiting to talk. No "you should just…" advice. They just sat with you. Heard you. Let you be.

Felt different, didn't it? Like for a moment, you weren't carrying it all alone.

That's what empathy does. It says: I see you. I hear you. You matter.

Strong men don't just take up space—they make space. They pay attention. They lean in. They leave people feeling lighter.

The kind of man who listens—who truly sees people—builds relationships that last. Because when people feel safe to be themselves around you, trust isn't just given. It's earned.

ACTION CHALLENGE

Step 1: Listen with Intention.

Pick someone in your life who could use a moment of empathy.

Instead of asking, "How are you?" ask, "What's been on your mind lately?"

Then lean in—listen without interrupting, fixing, or judging.

Step 2: Reflect on What You Learn.

After your conversation, write down one key thing you learned about them.

Keep it in mind for future interactions—this builds trust and deepens connection.

FINAL TAKEAWAY

Strong men don't just talk—they listen.

Empathy isn't about fixing. It's about understanding.

And when you lead with presence, you don't just strengthen your relationships—you sharpen the man you're becoming.

DAY 43

BOUNDARIES AREN'T BARRIERS—THEY'RE BRIDGES

If you're the one everyone depends on—the go-to guy—setting boundaries can feel wrong. You've been told that a good man is always available. Always sacrificing. Always putting others first.

But let's get real: without boundaries, you're not actually helping. You're just running yourself into the ground.

YOUR RESENTMENT IS A WARNING SIGN

Think about that frustration you feel when you say "yes" but want to say "no." That slow, quiet resentment creeping in? That's your soul waving a red flag. It's telling you: You're giving away parts of yourself that you can't afford to lose.

Boundaries aren't about shutting people out. They're about protecting your time, your energy, and your peace—so you can show up fully, not halfway.

Take a moment. Where are your boundaries thin? Where are you giving too much? Where do you feel drained instead of fulfilled? Who in your life takes but never pours back into you?

If you're constantly running on empty, that's not selflessness—it's self-neglect. And over time, that catches up with you.

ACTION CHALLENGE

Step 1: Identify Your Weakest Boundary.

Write down one area in your life where you've been saying "yes" too often.

Now, decide on one thing to say "no" to this week.

Examples:

- Declining a favor you don't have the capacity for.
- Not answering a call during your downtime.
- Turning down a request that drains you.

Step 2: Practice Your Boundary Language.

Decide how you'll communicate your boundary—without guilt.

Try saying:

- "I can't commit to this right now."
- "I need to focus on myself, so I'm going to pass."
- "I appreciate you asking, but I have to decline."

The ones who truly respect you will respect your boundaries too.

FINAL TAKEAWAY

Not everyone will like your boundaries. Let them be uncomfortable.

The people who love you will respect your limits—even if it takes time.

The ones who only loved your availability won't.

Protecting your peace doesn't make you selfish—it makes you sustainable.

You're not here to be used up.

You're here to be whole.

DAY 44

SAY WHAT NEEDS TO BE SAID

Communication isn't just about talking—it's about being real. Saying what you mean. Meaning what you say.

But too often, we bite our tongues. We don't want to seem too emotional. Come off as needy. Be a burden.

So, we swallow the words and tell ourselves, It's not that deep. I'll just keep it to myself.

But the words you don't say don't disappear. They get buried. They turn into frustration. They harden into resentment. And over time, they build walls between you and the people who matter most.

THE CONVERSATIONS I AVOIDED

For a long time, I kept everything inside. Not because I didn't have anything to say—but because I didn't know how to say it. I'd hold it in and think, What's the point? Nobody's gonna get it anyway.

I told myself I was protecting myself. I told myself I was keeping the peace. But what I was really doing? Isolating myself.

Then one day, someone close to me said, "I never know what you're really thinking."

And that hit me—because I wanted to be understood. But how could anyone understand me if I never let them in?

So, I started speaking up. Just a little at first. And what I learned changed everything:

Honesty isn't a burden—it's a bridge.

ACTION CHALLENGE

Step 1: Identify the Unspoken Words.

Think about one relationship where unspoken words have built a wall.

Write down one thing you've been holding back.

Start with:

- "I feel..."
- "I need..."

Step 2: Initiate the Conversation.

It doesn't have to be perfect—just honest.

Start small if you need to.

- Focus on how you feel instead of blaming or criticizing.
- Keep it simple, but real.

FINAL TAKEAWAY

Silence doesn't keep the peace—it keeps you disconnected.

Honesty doesn't mean saying everything. It means saying what matters.

The words you hold back build walls. The words you speak build connection.

Say what needs to be said—before the chance to say it is gone.

DAY 45

YOUR PARTNER SHOULD BE YOUR BEST FRIEND

Love is powerful.

But without friendship, love alone won't hold a relationship together.

Beyond attraction. Beyond shared responsibilities.

It's the little moments of connection that truly matter.

THE SHIFT FROM LOVE TO ROUTINE

Think back to the beginning—before life got hectic.

The inside jokes. The late-night convos. The way you could just enjoy each other's company.

Back then, there wasn't a schedule to manage, bills to pay, or responsibilities weighing you down.

But over time, life crowds in. Conversations turn into checklists. Date nights fade. The laughter gets quiet.

And it's not because the love is gone—it's because the friendship stopped being a priority.

THE MOMENT WE REALIZED WE WERE ON AUTOPILOT

There came a point when my wife and I had to check ourselves.

Somewhere along the way, we slipped into autopilot. Conversations weren't deep anymore—they were about groceries, calendars, and who was doing what.

We weren't laughing like we used to. We weren't having fun just to have fun.

And it wasn't about a lack of love. It was a lack of intention.

So, we made a choice: stop treating fun like a luxury—and start treating it like a necessity.

Nothing big. Just small moments that made us feel like us again.

Playing video games together. Sending funny reels during the day.

Sitting in the car, listening to music, just vibing.

That shift changed everything.

THE TRUTH ABOUT LASTING LOVE

A relationship without friendship is just a partnership. And that's not enough.

You need to laugh together. Be silly together. Enjoy each other—outside of survival mode.

Passion fades. Responsibilities build. But friendship?

That's what keeps love from breaking under the weight.

So today, do something small but intentional.

Bring back the energy of: "I just love being around you."

ACTION CHALLENGE

Step 1: Plan an Intentional Moment of Fun with Your Partner Today.

- Cook dinner together.
- Play a game.
- Send them a funny meme.

Do anything that reminds you both that love isn't just about effort—it's about joy.

Step 2: Go Deeper.

Ask your partner:

"What do you miss most about the early days of our relationship?"

Use their answer as inspiration to recreate or bring back some of those moments this week.

FINAL TAKEAWAY

Love isn't just about what you build—it's about what you enjoy.

Don't just do life together. Have fun in it.

Friendship is the glue that keeps love strong.

So make it a priority. Protect it. Feed it. Laugh often.

Because at the end of the day, your partner shouldn't just be the person you love. They should be the person you love doing life with.

PILLAR 4

OWNING YOUR POWER

(DAYS 46–73)

This phase is where understanding becomes action.

Up to this point, we've been laying the foundation—breaking down old patterns, building resilience, and shifting your mindset. But at some point, you have to stop just thinking about who you could be and start moving like him.

This is where you take everything you've learned and put it to work.

WHAT IT MEANS TO OWN YOUR POWER

Owning your power means taking full responsibility for the choices that shape your life. It's about showing up with clarity, courage, and intention.

It means:

- Defining success on your own terms.
- Following your passions with purpose.
- Taking bold steps to become the man you were built to be.

For many of us, that shift isn't easy. We've been conditioned to play it safe. To follow a script we didn't write. To shrink ourselves to fit into someone else's expectations.

But if you want something different, you have to start moving like the man who already has it.

THE RISK OF STAYING THE SAME

Yes, it's uncomfortable to take control. But staying stuck just because it's familiar? That's riskier.

I've had to bet on myself when everything was on the line—when the odds weren't in my favor. And it was in those uncertain, uncomfortable moments that everything shifted.

That's what I want for you: a life you're proud of. One you built with your own hands, your own choices, and your own conviction.

WHAT'S AHEAD IN THIS PHASE

In this phase, we're going to:

- Dismantle the limiting beliefs that keep you playing small.
- Define your purpose and reconnect with what lights you up.
- Build the discipline to stay grounded when life pushes back.

Because real power isn't loud—it's consistent. It's not just dreaming big—it's staying steady when it gets hard. You have to be willing to take the risks that actually matter.

That means:

- Getting uncomfortable.
- Making bold decisions.
- Walking with confidence—even before you feel ready.

Success isn't about what the world sees—it's about whether your life reflects who you really are. That includes how you lead, how you love, and how you show up for the people who count on you.

This phase is about becoming the man who owns his story—not the one who lets life write it for him.

MOVE LIKE THE MAN YOU'RE BECOMING

This is your moment. To step up. To take action. To live boldly.

No more waiting. No more shrinking.

Let's move.

DAY 46

REDEFINE SUCCESS ON YOUR TERMS

Success. Everybody talks about it, chases it, measures it. But when was the last time you actually stopped to ask yourself—what does success really mean to me?

For too long, we've been handed a script: money, power, status. The right title. The right house. The right image. But chasing someone else's dream will leave you exhausted, running in circles, wondering why none of it ever feels like enough.

THE ILLUSION OF SUCCESS

Be real with yourself—how many times have you scrolled through social media, seen someone else's life, and felt like you were behind?

Maybe it's the friend with the six-figure salary. Or the guy posting luxury trips, watches, and cars. But what you're seeing? That's not the full story.

I used to think success was about numbers—dollars in the bank, promotions on my résumé, the kind of car I drove. But when I hit a low point—grinding nonstop and still feeling like I was failing my family—it hit me: I wasn't chasing my dream. I was chasing theirs.

And the success I really wanted? It looked nothing like what I thought.

It looked like:

- Presence.

- Peace.
- Purpose.

It looked like being there for my family. Waking up with clarity. Being proud of the man I was becoming. That shift changed everything.

ACTION CHALLENGE

Step 1: Identify Your Fulfillment Moments.

Take five minutes to reflect on the moments that made you feel most fulfilled in the past year.

Write them down and note what those moments had in common.

Step 2: Break Free from the Script.

Identify one way you've been chasing someone else's definition of success—whether it's material, professional, or social.

Decide on one small change you can make this week to prioritize what matters most to you.

FINAL TAKEAWAY

Your definition of success will grow as you do. What mattered at 25 might mean nothing at 40—and that's not failure. That's growth.

Success isn't about proving anything. It's about aligning your life with your values, day by day. Forget their rules. Define your own.

And then live like you mean it.

DAY 47

TEAR UP THE SCRIPT

From the moment we're old enough to understand the world, we're handed a role to play. Be the provider. Be strong. Don't show weakness. Climb the ladder. Win at all costs.

But who wrote that script? And why do we keep following it when it doesn't even feel like us?

BREAKING FREE FROM THE PRESSURE

It's easy to get caught in the pressure. The friend flexing his new car. The coworker bragging about his next big move. The family members who only seem proud when you hit another milestone.

But just because everyone else is running the same race doesn't mean you have to. Success isn't one-size-fits-all.

Maybe for you, success looks like becoming the kind of father you never had. Maybe it's choosing peace over pressure. Purpose over applause.

Breaking free from what the world expects of you isn't easy. It takes courage to say, "That's not for me." But think about what it's costing you to live a life that doesn't feel like yours—the stress, the numbness, the feeling that you're always behind.

Is keeping up the act really worth the price?

ACTION CHALLENGE

Step 1: Expose the Script.

Write down three expectations you've been following that don't actually align with who you are.

Ask yourself:

- Where did this belief come from?
- Have I been following this out of obligation or true desire?

Step 2: Rewrite It.

Take one of those expectations and flip it into a truth that actually fits you.

Examples:

✘ Old script: "A real man works 24/7 and never slows down."

✔ New truth: "A real man creates a life that allows him to be fully present."

✘ Old script: "Success means having the biggest house and the best title."

✔ New truth: "Success means building a life that aligns with my values."

Step 3: Take One Bold Step Today.

Choose one way to live by your rewritten truth:

- Say no to something that isn't for you.
- Say yes to something that is.
- Take one step toward a goal that actually matters to YOU—not anyone else.

FINAL TAKEAWAY

You don't have to live by a script that was never written for you.

You don't have to prove anything to anyone.

You're allowed to redefine what success means for you—and start writing a story you actually want to live.

DAY 48

SET GOALS THAT FEEL LIKE HOME

When was the last time you set a goal that truly felt like yours?

Not something society convinced you to chase. Not the promotion they said would make you whole. Not the car, the title, or the picture-perfect life. But a goal that lit something up inside you. A goal that felt like home.

ARE YOUR GOALS TRULY YOURS?

Too often, we spend our lives chasing what looks good on paper—only to end up burned out, disconnected, and unfulfilled. We hit the milestone but still feel empty. Because those goals weren't built from truth—they were built from pressure.

Your goals should reflect what actually matters to you: your values, your passions, your growth. When your goals come from outside voices, they wear you down. But when they're rooted in who you are, they fill you up. They don't just push you—they pull you. And they keep you moving, not because you have to... but because you want to.

ACTION CHALLENGE

Step 1: Identify Authentic Goals.

Write down three goals that truly reflect your values and passions—

Goals that energize you, not ones that just look good on paper.

Step 2: Take the First Step.

Choose one of the goals and write down a small, actionable step you can take today.

It could be something as simple as:

- Making a phone call.
- Blocking off time on your calendar.
- Doing research on your next move.

FINAL TAKEAWAY

You define what success means.

You decide what matters.

Build a life that feels like it belongs to you—not one that just looks good from the outside.

DAY 49

ROADBLOCKS AREN'T THE END—THEY'RE THE TRAINING GROUND

Life isn't a smooth highway. It's a rough, unpredictable road—full of potholes, detours, and stop signs you never saw coming.

Some days, it feels like just when you start making progress, something knocks you off course. It's frustrating. It's exhausting. And if we're keeping it real? Sometimes it makes you want to throw your hands up and walk away.

But hear this: roadblocks don't define your journey—they shape your endurance.

Every setback gave you something, even if you couldn't see it in the moment.

Losing that job? It taught you how to pivot. That breakup? It showed you what you need, what you won't tolerate, and how to stand on your own. That failure? It wasn't the end—it was a lesson that refined your game.

The road you've traveled has trained you.

The detours taught you discipline.

The delays developed your resilience.

You're not behind. You've been in training. And every mile has made you stronger.

ACTION CHALLENGE

Step 1: Name the Roadblock.

Write down the roadblock you're currently facing, whether it's financial, emotional, or situational. Seeing it clearly will help you take the first step forward.

Step 2: Build Your Strategy.

Write down one specific action you can take today to start moving through the roadblock. It could be calling a trusted mentor, setting up a budget, or carving out time for a skill you need to refine.

Step 3: Lean Into Support.

Identify one person in your corner who can support or encourage you in this moment. Reach out to them—whether it's a quick call or simply letting them know what you're going through.

And hear me on this—you're not built to carry it all alone. Lean on your people. Family, friends, mentors—whatever your support system looks like, use it. There's no strength in suffering in silence.

Roadblocks aren't here to stop you. They're here to sharpen you. Every challenge you push through adds to your story, making you stronger, sharper, and more prepared for the life you're meant to build.

DAY 50

THE STRENGTH OF STILLNESS—HOW TO STOP RUNNING FROM YOURSELF

Most men don't sit in silence long enough to hear what their own soul is trying to say.

Instead, we stay busy. We work. We grind. We keep moving. Because stopping? That's when the thoughts catch up to us. That's when the silence gets loud.

So, we fill it—scrolling, streaming, staying on the go. Anything to avoid sitting still long enough to feel what's really going on inside. To avoid the emotions we've buried. To avoid the weight we don't want to carry.

But here's what you need to understand: What you keep avoiding in the silence is what's been keeping you stuck.

THE MOMENT I REALIZED I HAD BEEN RUNNING FROM MYSELF

For a long time, I kept moving. I told myself it was about being productive. About grinding. About building something real.

But if I'm honest, I was afraid of what would happen if I stopped. Because every time I slowed down, the silence got louder—and I didn't want to hear what it had to say.

It wasn't until I had no choice—until life forced me to stop—that I finally faced it. The emotions I'd buried. The wounds I hadn't fully healed from. The pressure I didn't even know I was carrying.

Stillness isn't weakness. It's strength. Sitting with yourself. Being present. Actually listening to what's inside of you. That's where clarity begins. That's where healing starts.

ACTION CHALLENGE

Step 1: Create Five Minutes of Stillness.

Today, take just five minutes to sit in complete stillness.

No phone.

No distractions.

No noise.

Just you, your thoughts, and whatever comes up.

Step 2: Ask Yourself One Question.

After a few minutes of silence, ask: "What have I been avoiding?"

Write down the first thing that comes to mind.

It might be a feeling you haven't processed.

It might be a truth you haven't faced.

It might be something you've known deep down but haven't admitted to yourself yet.

Whatever it is—name it. Because once you name it, you can face it.

FINAL TAKEAWAY

Busyness can be a form of avoidance. Stillness isn't about stopping—it's about listening.

You can't outrun yourself forever. The only way forward is through.

Sit with yourself today. You might finally hear the part of you that's been waiting to speak.

DAY 51

KNOW YOUR WHY, LIVE YOUR TRUTH

Why do you get up in the morning? What pulls you forward when life feels heavy and the grind wears you down?

If you've never really thought about it, you're not alone. A lot of us spend years chasing things that don't actually move us—hustling for goals that were never really ours in the first place.

But without a clear why, you're just running. No finish line. No real direction. Just motion without meaning.

Your why isn't about what the world tells you should matter. It's about what sets your soul on fire. What gives you energy. What makes you feel like you're exactly where you're meant to be.

It might be the family you're building, the impact you're making, or the dream you refuse to let die. It's that thing that reminds you why quitting isn't an option.

FINDING THE WHY THAT DRIVES YOU

Think back to the moments that made you feel fully alive. Maybe it was watching your kids grow. Creating something that mattered. Showing up for someone when they needed you most.

Your why is usually connected to the legacy you want to leave behind. And when you start living with that in mind, you don't just change your life—you change the lives of everyone around you.

ACTION CHALLENGE

Step 1: Define Your Why.

Spend five minutes writing down the moments that made you feel most alive—

Times when you felt:

- Fulfilled.
- Energized.
- Deeply connected.

What were you doing? Who were you with?

Step 2: Align Your Day.

Choose one small action you can take today that honors your why.

It could be:

- Spending quality time with a loved one.
- Working toward a personal goal.
- Saying no to something that doesn't serve your purpose.

FINAL TAKEAWAY

Living with purpose doesn't mean you always have clarity. It means you always have a reason to keep going.

Your why is your fuel when the fire runs low. It's your compass when the path gets unclear. It's your anchor when life gets loud.

Don't waste your energy chasing what doesn't fulfill you.

Live for what sets your soul on fire.

DAY 52

OWN YOUR LIFE, OWN YOUR CHOICES

When you look in the mirror today, remember this: you're the one who has to live with your choices every day. Life's too short to live on someone else's terms.

Every man knows what it feels like to point fingers—to blame the timing, the situation, or the people who didn't show up for us. Maybe you've told yourself, "If things had gone differently…" or "If they had backed me, I'd be further along." But blame doesn't build the life you want. Every second spent blaming is a second you're not building.

Taking responsibility isn't about beating yourself up for what didn't work—it's about standing up and saying, "This is my life. And I'm done letting outside forces write my story."

Imagine the power in that. Imagine the freedom in deciding you're done just surviving—and you're ready to thrive.

So be honest: What's one area of your life where you've been playing it safe? Work? Health? Your relationships? What excuse have you been holding onto? And more importantly—are you ready to let it go?

I know what it feels like to be cornered by circumstances. When my company shut down, I had two options: take a demotion or bet on myself. Betting on myself was terrifying—but it's the choice that put my future back in my own hands.

That's what it means to own your life. You move forward, even when the path isn't clear. You don't need to have all the answers. Ownership doesn't mean perfection—it means showing up, doing the work, and refusing to let fear do the talking.

You're not stuck—you're in charge.

ACTION CHALLENGE

Step 1: Face the Excuses.

Identify one area of your life where you've been avoiding responsibility.

Write down the excuses you've been telling yourself. Seeing them in black and white can help you recognize what's holding you back.

Step 2: Make a Move.

Take one bold step today to own that area of your life.

It could mean:

- Initiating a difficult conversation.
- Committing to a new routine.
- Setting a non-negotiable boundary.

Whatever it is, do it with intention and take control.

DAY 53

CHASING WHAT SETS YOUR SOUL ON FIRE

Ever catch yourself wondering, "Am I really living… or just existing?"

It's easy to get stuck in the cycle—grinding through work, showing up for everyone else, checking all the boxes—only to end the day feeling empty. Maybe you're successful on paper, but something still feels off. Like a part of you is missing.

Living for someone else's version of success will drain you faster than any struggle ever could.

Your purpose isn't about meeting expectations. It's about doing what makes you feel alive.

Think back to the last time you lost track of time doing something you loved. That spark? That's your North Star. And it's been waiting on you to follow it.

THE FIRST STEP TOWARD PURPOSE

Finding purpose doesn't mean dropping everything overnight. It starts with small, intentional moves. It starts with permission.

Maybe it's picking up that thing you used to love. Maybe it's trying something new. Maybe it's just pausing long enough to ask yourself, "What do I actually want?"

Your purpose isn't some far-off destination. It's in the moments that light you up now.

The more you lean into those moments, the clearer the path becomes.

ACTION CHALLENGE

Step 1: Discover the Spark.

Write down three things or activities that make you lose track of time.

Don't overthink it—just focus on what lights you up.

Step 2: Take a Step Toward Passion.

Choose one of those things and find a way to incorporate it into your day.

Examples:

- If you love music, spend 10 minutes listening to or creating it.

- If you're energized by helping others, look for an opportunity to support someone in need.

- If you've been wanting to explore something new, take a small step like watching a tutorial or signing up for a class.

DAY 54

BRING BACK THE FIRE YOU LOST (IT'S STILL IN YOU)

Life can wear you down in ways you never expected. The long hours. The constant demands. The weight of being everything for everyone. And somewhere in all that pressure, the fire you once had—the one that made you feel alive—starts to dim. Sometimes so much, you wonder if it's even still there.

But let me tell you this: it didn't die. It's still there. Waiting. Waiting for you to stop ignoring it. To stop letting life bury it beneath obligation, pressure, and survival mode.

RECONNECTING WITH WHAT MAKES YOU COME ALIVE

Think back to when you were a kid. What lit you up? What made you lose track of time?

Before the bills. Before the responsibilities. Before the world told you to "be realistic"—there was something that pulled you in. That part of you? It never left. You just stopped giving it room to breathe.

Passion isn't a luxury—it's fuel. When you reconnect with what excites you, life stops feeling like a checklist and starts feeling like a calling. And this isn't about being great at something. It's about remembering what it feels like to be fully awake.

Now imagine what life could look like if you gave yourself permission to step back into what you love. Not for money. Not for validation. Just because it makes you feel alive again.

ACTION CHALLENGE

Step 1: Spark the Flame.

Think of one passion or activity that used to bring you joy but has been buried under life's demands.

Take a small action to reconnect with it today.

Examples:

- Loved painting? Grab a napkin or a piece of paper and draw something small.
- Miss playing sports? Spend 5 minutes shooting hoops or tossing a ball around.
- Loved exploring? Take a walk somewhere new or look up a topic that excites you.

Step 2: Reclaim Your Time.

Look at your schedule and block out just 15 minutes this week to do something purely for yourself—no obligations, no expectations.

Even small windows can reignite your fire.

FINAL TAKEAWAY

Give yourself grace. You're not the same man who first fell in love with that thing—and that's not a bad thing. Now you've got more depth. More scars. More wisdom. More soul.

This isn't about going backward. It's about moving forward—with the part of you that's always been real.

You weren't built to just survive.

You were made to shine.

DAY 55

THE COST OF BEING A LONE WOLF – WHY BROTHERHOOD MATTERS

Most men move through life like lone wolves—handling everything alone, carrying the weight in silence, convinced no one else would understand. Maybe you've told yourself: "I don't need anyone. I got this." "Talking won't change anything." "I don't want to burden anyone with my problems."

But here's the thing: lions move in prides. Wolves hunt in packs. But men? We've been conditioned to go solo. And it's killing us.

THE TRUTH ABOUT DOING IT ALONE

For years, I handled everything on my own. I told myself that was strength. That needing help meant I was slipping. That I was better off figuring it out by myself.

But I was exhausted. I was carrying weight I didn't need to carry, struggling in silence, and pushing away the very people who wanted to walk with me.

The moment I stopped isolating myself, everything changed. I had men who held me accountable. Friends who called out my blind spots and helped me grow. A circle that didn't just comfort me—they challenged me to rise.

What most men don't realize is this: There's strength in standing alone. But there's power in standing together.

ACTION CHALLENGE

Step 1: Identify Your Lone Wolf Mentality.

Think about an area of your life where you've been trying to handle everything alone.

Write it down.

- Work stress?
- A personal struggle?
- Something you've convinced yourself no one else would understand?

Step 2: Reach Out to Someone.

Choose one person you trust—a friend, mentor, or even a peer—and initiate a real conversation.

- Send a text.
- Set up a time to talk.
- Simply say, "Hey, I've been holding a lot in, and I want to start talking about it."

You don't have to spill everything. Just start

FINAL TAKEAWAY

You weren't built to do life alone.

Independence is valuable—but isolation will break you.

Brotherhood doesn't make you weak. It makes you dangerous in the right way.

You don't have to carry everything by yourself.

Find your people.

Build your circle.

Let them in.

DAY 56

QUIT WAITING—BRING YOUR PASSIONS TO LIFE

Knowing what fires you up is one thing. Doing something about it? That's the game-changer. Dreams without action are just ideas collecting dust. And ideas don't change your life—movement does.

The real question isn't whether you have a passion. It's whether you're going to stop waiting and start moving.

How many times have you told yourself, "I'll start when things calm down," or "Now's just not the right time"? Life doesn't slow down—it stacks up. And every time you push your passions to the side, you starve a part of yourself that needs to breathe.

The things that light you up? They're not just hobbies. They're fuel. They remind you who you are beneath the grind.

So today, I'm calling you out: No more waiting.

Start small if you need to. But start.

ACTION CHALLENGE

Step 1: Take the First Step.

Pick one passion you've been putting off and take a single, specific step toward it today.

Examples:

- Sketch out your business idea.
- Write the first paragraph of your book.
- Call a friend to brainstorm.

Step 2: Plan Ahead.

Set aside time in your calendar for this passion over the next week.

Protect that time like an appointment.

Consistency, even in small bursts, builds momentum.

FINAL TAKEAWAY

This isn't about perfection. It's about movement.

Every step you take toward your passion is a step toward a fuller, more honest life.

Celebrate the small wins—they're proof that you're in motion.

Your dream doesn't belong on pause.

It belongs in your hands.

Start now.

DAY 57

OWN THE LIFE YOU WERE MADE FOR

Purpose isn't just some nice idea—it's the fire behind every move that matters. It's what keeps you going when quitting would be easier. It's what holds you steady when life hits hard. But purpose isn't handed to you. It's something you rise into.

Think about the last time you felt fully alive. Was it a moment with your kids? A project that pulled you in so deep you forgot to check the time? Helping someone who needed you? Those moments aren't just feel-good highlights—they're clues. Signals pointing to what makes you come alive.

Purpose doesn't always show up in some big, dramatic revelation. Most of the time, it's already there—hiding in plain sight. In the things that make you feel whole. In the things you'd do even if nobody ever said thank you.

But owning your purpose takes courage. It means being honest about what drives you—even if it doesn't match the world's definition of success. The world will try to sell you a script. Rip it up. Your life isn't a performance. It's a mission.

You weren't made to fit in. You were made to light something up.

ACTION CHALLENGE

Step 1: Look for Patterns.

Reflect on three moments in your life when you felt most alive—when time seemed to disappear, and you were fully in the moment.

Write them down and identify what those moments have in common.

Step 2: Make Space.

Pick one activity from your list that fuels your purpose and schedule time for it this week.

Treat it like an unbreakable appointment with yourself.

Examples:

- Spending time with your kids.
- Working on a project that excites you.
- Helping someone in need.

FINAL TAKEAWAY

You're not waiting for permission. You don't need a green light or anyone's approval. This is your life. Your mission. Your lane. Own it—and walk like it already belongs to you.

DAY 58

STOP WAITING—MOVE NOW

How many times have you told yourself, "I'll start tomorrow"?

How many dreams have you talked about but never chased?

How many goals are still sitting in the back of your mind, gathering dust?

Passion without action is just noise. The fire inside you fades if you don't feed it.

It's easy to get comfortable—caught in routines, letting days blur into weeks, and weeks into years. But life won't wait.

Comfort is a silent thief. It robs you of your potential while convincing you that you're safe. Every man knows that pull—to stay where it's familiar, avoid the risk, and put off the uncomfortable work of moving forward.

But what's familiar might be what's keeping you stuck. And the cost of staying still is far greater than the fear of failure.

WHAT'S HOLDING YOU BACK?

Is it fear of judgment? Fear of falling short?

Doubt is loud—but it's not the truth.

Every man you admire started where you are—unsure, questioning himself, wondering if he had what it took.

The difference? He moved anyway.

Failure isn't the end. It's the teacher.

Falling forward is still progress.

But standing still? That's the only way you lose.

ACTION CHALLENGE

Step 1: Start with One.

Choose ONE goal or dream you've been putting off.

Break it into the smallest possible step you can take today.

Examples:

- Send one email.
- Research one resource.
- Commit one hour to it.

Step 2: Build Accountability.

Share your goal with someone you trust—a friend, partner, or mentor.

Ask them to check in with you about your progress or share your step for the day with them to solidify your commitment.

FINAL TAKEAWAY

You're not alone in this. Every man stands at the crossroads of comfort and change.

This moment is yours.

The choice you make today can shift your entire future.

Action is what separates the dreamers from the doers.

Don't wait for perfect conditions. Don't wait for confidence.

Move now.

DAY 59

MORE THAN JUST EXISTING

Have you ever stopped to ask yourself—why am I really here? Beyond the routines, the bills, the grind—what's the deeper reason you wake up every morning?

Every man has a purpose. But too often, it gets buried—under pressure, self-doubt, and the noise of daily life.

Purpose isn't just about what you do. It's about who you are—and the mark you leave behind. It's what keeps you going when life gets heavy. That quiet voice inside that says, "You were built for more."

Maybe you've caught glimpses of it—the fire that lights up when you talk about what truly matters, the cause you'd stand for no matter the odds.

The first step to walking in your purpose is getting real with yourself.

What moves you?

What impact do you want your life to leave?

These answers don't live in titles, paychecks, or other people's approval. They live in what makes your life feel full. Whole. Meaningful.

And here's what you need to know—your purpose is directly tied to your legacy.

Legacy isn't about how much you stacked in the bank or what positions you held.

It's about how you showed up.

It's the way you made people feel.

It's the wisdom you passed down.

It's the lives you lifted just by being you.

Imagine someone telling your story years from now. What will they say? Will they talk about a man who lived with intention? Who stood for something bigger than himself? Who made a difference in the lives around him?

You don't find purpose by waiting.

You build it—through presence, through courage, through action.

ACTION CHALLENGE

Step 1: Define Your Legacy.

Write a one-sentence legacy statement:

_"I want to be remembered as the man who _____."

Let it reflect the values and impact that matter most to you.

Step 2: Align Your Actions.

Identify one small action you can take today that aligns with your legacy statement.

Examples:

- If your legacy is about kindness, choose one person to help today.

- If your legacy is about leadership, offer mentorship or guidance to someone who could use your support.

Living with purpose doesn't mean you have all the answers.

It means committing to the journey, choosing to show up, and letting your actions reflect what matters most.

Stop waiting for the right time. Start today.

DAY 60

FEAR ISN'T A STOP SIGN—IT'S A SHARPENING TOOL

You know that moment when the "what ifs" start swarming your mind like a storm?

What if I fail? What if I look foolish? What if I'm not as ready as I thought?

Fear has a way of sneaking in and freezing you up—before you even take the first step. It makes small risks feel massive. It convinces you that staying where you are is safer than trying and falling short.

But fear isn't your enemy. It's a signal. A test. A sharpening tool. Every man who's ever built something meaningful has felt fear breathing down his neck. They didn't wait for it to leave—they moved through it.

Those "what ifs" didn't stop them. They fueled them.

Failure wasn't the finish line—it was part of the blueprint. Every stumble taught something. Every misstep added grit. The men who shift culture, who change the game—they're not the ones who dodge fear. They're the ones who face it and level up because of it.

ACTION CHALLENGE

Step 1: Identify the Fear.

Write down one fear that has been keeping you stagnant—something you've been avoiding because of the "what ifs."

Step 2: Take the First Step.

Break the fear into small, manageable steps. Then, commit to taking just one step today, no matter how small.

Examples:

- Afraid to start a project? Spend 10 minutes planning the first move.
- Nervous about a conversation? Write down what you want to say.
- Avoiding a decision? Pick one small action that will move you closer to clarity.

FINAL TAKEAWAY

Whatever it is—move.

Fear doesn't get the final say—your action does.

Courage isn't the absence of fear. It's choosing to show up anyway.

And right now?

It's your move.

DAY 61

PROCRASTINATION IS ROBBING YOU—TIME TO FIGHT BACK

Procrastination is that smooth talker convincing you there's always more time.

"You'll get to it tomorrow," it whispers. But then tomorrow comes—and somehow, the list only gets longer.

It's not about laziness. It's about the weight of starting. The longer you wait, the heavier it gets—until just thinking about it drains your energy and your confidence.

We've all been there. Maybe it's scrolling your phone. Maybe it's busying yourself with everything except what actually needs to get done. It feels like a break, but deep down, you know it's just delay. And that unfinished task? It doesn't go away. It lingers—adding quiet stress and keeping you stuck.

BREAKING FREE STARTS HERE

Procrastination doesn't just steal time. It hijacks your momentum. It clutters your mind. It keeps you circling the same mountain, wondering why nothing's changing.

So, ask yourself: What are you really avoiding?

The pressure to get it perfect?

The fear of messing it up?

Not knowing where to begin?

Whatever it is, name it. Because once you call it out, you can call yourself up. And that's how you take your power back.

ACTION CHALLENGE

Step 1: Call It Out.

Write down one task you've been avoiding.

Underneath it, write the reason why—fear, overwhelm, or just not knowing where to start.

Naming it takes away its power.

Step 2: Start the Clock.

Set a timer for just 10 minutes and commit to starting the task.

Don't worry about finishing—just focus on moving.

Examples:

- If it's a big work project, spend 10 minutes organizing your notes.
- If it's a phone call, draft a quick script or outline what you want to say.
- If it's an overdue chore, pick one small piece of it to tackle.

FINAL TAKEAWAY

Every time you choose action over avoidance, you're proving to yourself that you're not a man who stays stuck—you're a man who handles his business.

One step at a time. One decision at a time. That's how you build the habit of progress. That's how you become the man you know you're capable of being.

The man you want to be?

He's on the other side of procrastination.

Start today.

DAY 62

BREAK FREE FROM THE WALLS HOLDING YOU BACK

Some days, it feels like you're boxed in—trapped inside limits you didn't even realize you set. Maybe those walls started as protection from pain or failure. But over time, they've turned into a prison—keeping you stuck, disconnected, and far from the life you actually want.

Fear of judgment. Past mistakes. Self-doubt. Brick by brick, it all stacks up until it feels like there's no way out.

But listen—those walls aren't as solid as they seem. They're not built from truth. They're built from wounds you've outgrown and fears that no longer serve you.

Just because you've been hurt before doesn't mean you're meant to repeat the cycle. Strength doesn't come from staying hidden behind the walls. It comes from tearing them down—and stepping into the man you're becoming.

WHAT'S BEEN BOXING YOU IN?

Fear of failure? It's keeping you from taking the risk.

Pride? It's stopping you from asking for help.

The pressure to look like you've got it all together? That's keeping you from being real.

Whatever it is—call it out. Naming your walls isn't weakness. It's the first step to freedom.

ACTION CHALLENGE:

Action #1:

Name the Wall. Write down one "wall" that's been keeping you boxed in. Examples: fear of judgment, perfectionism, or the need to handle everything alone. Ask yourself: What's this wall costing me?

Action #2:

Take a Swing. Commit to one small action today that chips away at the wall. Examples:

- If fear of failure is the wall, take a risk—big or small—and remind yourself that failure is part of growth.

- If pride is the wall, ask for help with one thing you've been struggling with.

- If perfectionism is the wall, complete a task and remind yourself that done is better than perfect.

Progress doesn't have to be big—but it does have to start. Even the smallest step forward is still forward.

You are not the walls you've built. You are the man with the courage to tear them down. And with every brick you remove, you're reclaiming the life you deserve. The freedom you're searching for? It's waiting on the other side. Take the first step.

FINAL TAKEAWAY

Progress doesn't have to be big—it just has to begin.

You are not the walls you built. You are the man with the courage to tear them down.

And with every brick you remove, you're reclaiming your life.

The freedom you've been looking for?

It's not gone. It's just waiting on the other side.

Take the step.

DAY 63

DROP THE WEIGHT AND MOVE FORWARD

Carrying the past is like walking through life with a weighted vest. Regrets. Grudges. Self-doubt. Each one adds another layer of weight. You might tell yourself holding onto them protects you—or maybe even fuels you. But the truth is, they're only slowing you down.

THE MOMENT I REALIZED I WAS HOLDING TOO MUCH

For years, I carried things I should've put down—pain from the past, unforgiveness, mistakes I kept replaying. I thought holding onto them made me stronger. I thought they'd keep me from getting hurt again. But all they did was drain me. Quietly. Constantly.

And when I finally let go? I didn't lose anything. I gained freedom.

Letting go isn't about pretending it didn't happen. It's about refusing to let it hold the pen while you write your next chapter.

ACTION CHALLENGE

Step 1: Identify Your Weight.

Write down one thing you're carrying that's weighing you down.

A grudge.

A regret.

A limiting belief.

Step 2: Create a Letting-Go Ritual.

Do something physical to symbolize releasing it:

- Rip up the piece of paper.
- Write it on a sticky note and throw it away.
- Burn it safely (if possible).

Seeing yourself physically let go makes it real.

FINAL TAKEAWAY

Letting go isn't weakness—it's wisdom. You don't move forward by dragging the past behind you. You move by releasing what no longer serves you.

You can't control what happened. But you can control what you carry.

Your next chapter isn't back there.

It's ahead.

Walk toward it—lighter, clearer, and free.

DAY 64

DOUBT IS LOUD, BUT IT'S NOT THE TRUTH

Doubt creeps in like an uninvited guest—whispering that you're not enough, that you don't have what it takes. It turns small decisions into mountains and keeps you stuck, second-guessing every move.

But doubt doesn't get the last word—you do.

Every man wrestles with doubt. Maybe it's wondering if you're enough for your family. Questioning whether you're doing enough at work. Feeling like you'll never measure up.

But doubt is a reaction—not reality.

Look back. You've made it through storms that should've taken you out. You're still here. Still standing. Still fighting. Doubt didn't stop you then—and it won't stop you now, unless you let it.

TALK BACK TO DOUBT

When doubt starts talking, don't just listen—talk back. Challenge it. Call it what it is. Think about a time you pushed through fear, stood up for yourself, or kept going when quitting would've been easier.

That's your proof.

You've done it before. You'll do it again.

ACTION CHALLENGE

Step 1: Talk Back to Doubt.

Write down one doubt that has been loud in your mind lately.

Then list three specific truths or moments that prove it wrong.

Examples:

- "I didn't think I could get through that tough project, but I did, and it turned out great."
- "I doubted I could handle fatherhood, but I show up every day for my family."
- "I thought I wasn't good enough to go after that opportunity, but I took the leap, and it worked out."

Step 2: Take One Bold Action.

Do something today that directly challenges that doubt:

- If you've doubted your voice, speak up in a conversation or meeting.
- If you've doubted your ability, start or finish a task you've been avoiding.
- If you've doubted your worth, remind yourself aloud: I've handled worse, and I'm stronger because of it.

FINAL TAKEAWAY

You've already overcome what once felt impossible. Doubt is just noise—it doesn't define you.

It never built anything worth remembering. But courage did.

You don't need all the answers—you just need the guts to keep going.

Trust your strength. Move with purpose. Let your actions shut doubt down.

DAY 65

SURROUND YOURSELF WITH MEN WHO MAKE YOU BETTER

No man is meant to walk this journey alone. But too many of us were taught to tough it out, to carry the weight without complaint, to deal with life in silence. We learned to wear isolation like it was strength.

But isolation isn't strength—it's a slow form of self-destruction. Life gets heavy, and having the right men in your corner isn't just helpful—it's necessary.

Even the strongest men need a tribe.

THE TRUTH ABOUT BROTHERHOOD

Take a hard look at your circle. Are the men around you helping you rise—or just keeping you comfortable where you are? Are they challenging you? Holding you accountable? Speaking truth when you need to hear it?

It's easy to confuse closeness with connection. Just because someone's in your life doesn't mean they're adding to it. Real brotherhood goes deeper than who you kick it with. You need men who sharpen you. Men who remind you of your purpose. Men who aren't afraid to call you higher—even when it's uncomfortable.

ACTION CHALLENGE

Step 1: Evaluate Your Circle.

Write down the names of three men who positively impact your life.

Ask yourself:

- What do they bring into my life?
- How do they challenge or support me?

Step 2: Strengthen the Bond.

Choose one of the three men and take an intentional step to connect with them today:

- Send a message to check in on them.
- Set up a time to meet for coffee or a meal.
- Express gratitude for their impact in your life.

FINAL TAKEAWAY

Your tribe isn't just a safety net—it's your mirror, your compass, your backbone when life hits hard. But here's the thing: you don't find that kind of brotherhood by accident.

You build it.

You show up. You pour in. You let yourself be seen. Because iron only sharpens iron when both are willing to be sharpened.

DAY 66

WHEN SHOWING UP CHANGES EVERYTHING

Life will hit you with moments that test everything—your strength, your patience, your character. Moments that make you want to pull back, avoid responsibility, and hope someone else will step in.

But real growth? Real leadership? That shows up when you do. Not when you step aside—but when you step forward.

THE POWER OF SHOWING UP

Think back to the last time you had to rise to the occasion. Maybe it was for your family. Maybe it was for a friend. Or maybe it was for yourself—on a day when doubt was creeping in and fear was louder than usual.

Those moments weren't convenient. And they definitely weren't easy.

But even when everything in you wanted to hesitate—you moved anyway. Fear might've whispered that you weren't ready, that you'd fail, that it wasn't your place.

But courage doesn't mean the fear goes away. It means you act in spite of it. And that's where real strength is built.

ACTION CHALLENGE

Step 1: Face the Call.

Think of one area in your life where you've been avoiding stepping up—whether it's a conversation, a responsibility, or a personal goal.

Write it down and commit to ONE specific step today.

Examples:

- Reach out to someone you've been avoiding.
- Set a time to address an issue you've been putting off.
- Take 15 minutes to begin tackling a task you've delayed.

Step 2: Celebrate the Small Wins.

At the end of the day, take a moment to reflect on what you did to show up.

Write down how it made you feel and the difference it created, no matter how small.

FINAL TAKEAWAY

Showing up isn't about having it all figured out. It's about refusing to sit on the sidelines of your own life. No one else can fight your battles for you, and life won't wait for you to feel 100% ready.

You've faced hard moments before—and you're still standing. That's not just survival. That's proof.

So today, step up. Answer the call. Walk in the strength of the man you're becoming.

DAY 67

WHEN LIFE HITS, HIT BACK HARDER

Life doesn't wait until you're ready before it throws a punch. One minute things feel steady—and the next, you're blindsided. A layoff. A betrayal. A loss so deep it rattles your soul.

Society loves to tell men to "man up," to shake it off like nothing happened. But some hits don't just sting. They knock the wind out of you. They make you question everything.

YOU ARE NOT BUILT TO STAY DOWN

The difference between staying broken and getting back up isn't about pretending you're okay—it's about what's still burning inside you. Not toughness. Not numbness. Not denial. But that deeper fire. That quiet refusal to quit. That part of you that says, "Not today. Not like this."

REMEMBER YOUR STRENGTH

Think back to the hardest moment you've ever faced. The kind of pain that made you want to throw in the towel. What kept you in the fight?

Was it the people who needed you?

The promise you made to yourself?

The belief—no matter how small—that you weren't done yet?

That's the part of you life is trying to break. And that's the part of you that needs to rise and fight back.

ACTION CHALLENGE

Step 1: Anchor Yourself.

Identify one thing or person that keeps you fighting—your family, your faith, a promise you made to yourself.

Write it down or find a physical object that symbolizes it (a photo, a note, a keepsake).

Keep it with you today as a reminder of why you don't quit.

Step 2: Take One Swing.

Think about an area of your life where life's hit you hard recently.

What's one action you can take today to swing back?

Examples:

- Make a call you've been avoiding.
- Write down a plan for how you're going to move forward.
- Take a moment to breathe and regroup—then get back in the fight.

FINAL TAKEAWAY

You don't need life to go easy. You just need to remember who you are.

Because no matter how hard life hits—you've got what it takes to hit back harder.

This isn't the end of your story.

Stand up. Swing back. Own the fight.

DAY 68

WHEN YOU FALL, GET UP STRONGER

Failure hits different when you've put your heart into something. It's not just about falling short—it can feel like a punch to the gut. Like a stamp on your worth as a man.

Society tells us to show off our wins and hide our losses. To walk like we've got it all together—even when we're falling apart.

But maybe we've been looking at it all wrong.

Failure isn't proof that you're not good enough. It's proof that you showed up. That you took a risk. That you had the courage to go after something that mattered.

Every man who's built something real has failed more times than he's succeeded. The difference? He didn't let failure write his final chapter.

Think back to a time when you gave something your all—and it still didn't work. Maybe you went after the promotion and got passed over. Maybe you tried to repair a relationship, but it still fell apart. That sting is real. But it's not the end.

Because the only thing failure really does is peel back the surface and show you what's underneath: your grit, your fight, your willingness to keep going.

And that's what makes you dangerous.

ACTION CHALLENGE

Step 1: Study the Fall.

Write down one failure that's been hard to let go of, and ask yourself:

- What did this experience teach me?
- What skill, strength, or resilience did I gain because of it?
- How can I use this lesson to move forward today?

Step 2: Build on the Lesson.

Take one action today based on what you learned from that failure.

Examples:

- If you failed because you weren't prepared, spend 10 minutes preparing for something ahead.
- If fear held you back, take one step toward the thing you're afraid of.
- If you chased the wrong goal, rewrite what success looks like to you now.

Resilience isn't built in the easy wins—it's forged in the hard losses. Failure is just a plot twist, not the end of the story.

DAY 69

THE FALL THAT BUILDS YOU – WHY FAILURE IS YOUR GREATEST TEACHER

Failure isn't just about falling—it's about what happens next. Because every man falls. The job that didn't work out. The relationship that fell apart. The moment you thought you had it figured out… until life proved otherwise. And in that moment, failure can feel like proof that you weren't good enough.

But failure isn't the final word—it's the foundation you build on.

FAILURE IS A CHOICE: STAY DOWN OR GET UP

Some men let failure define them. They fall, and instead of rising, they keep replaying the fall. They relive the mistake. They carry the shame. And after a while, they stop seeing the fall as something that happened—and start believing it's who they are.

But the strongest men aren't the ones who never fall. They're the ones who refuse to stay down.

ACTION CHALLENGE

Step 1: Reframe Your Last Fall.

Think about a failure you're still holding onto.

Write down:

- What you learned from it.
- How it redirected or strengthened you.
- One way you're stronger because of it today.

Step 2: Make Your Next Move.

Take an action that proves failure didn't break you.

Examples:

- If you hesitated to try again, make the first move.
- If you stopped believing in yourself, remind yourself why you started.
- If you've been stuck in fear, take the next step—imperfectly, but boldly.

FINAL TAKEAWAY

You don't grow when life is easy. You grow when you fall—and choose to rise anyway.

Failure isn't a dead end. It's a detour. A redirection toward who you're meant to become.

Your greatest comeback starts the moment you stop replaying the fall and decide to stand back up.

DAY 70

PERFECTION IS THE ENEMY OF PROGRESS—KEEP MOVING

From the time we're boys, we're fed this idea that being a man means getting everything right. No mistakes. No hesitation. No room to slip. We're taught to aim for perfection—like there's some invisible scoreboard tracking every move we make.

But here's what no one tells you: perfection is a lie. It's an exhausting, never-ending game you'll never win. Life doesn't reward flawless. It rewards effort. It rewards consistency. It rewards the man who keeps showing up, even when it's messy.

Maybe your career isn't where you thought it would be. Maybe your family life feels like controlled chaos on a good day. Maybe you've been waiting to feel "ready" before you make that next move.

But the truth? You'll never feel 100% ready. And if you keep waiting for perfect conditions, you'll be stuck waiting forever.

PROGRESS OVER PERFECTION

Think about where perfectionism has kept you stuck. Maybe it stopped you from applying for that job. Starting that business. Speaking up when it counted. Perfectionism doesn't make you excellent—it keeps you small.

The men who make an impact don't wait until everything is lined up just right. They move forward anyway—scars, uncertainty, and all.

ACTION CHALLENGE

Step 1: Pick One Imperfect Step.

Identify one thing you've been putting off because you don't feel "ready" or it doesn't feel "perfect."

Take one messy, imperfect step toward it today.

Examples:

- If it's a project, write down the first three steps and do one.

- If it's a difficult conversation, rehearse or send the first text to start it.

- If it's a goal, commit 15 minutes to work on it today—without worrying about getting it right.

Step 2: Celebrate Imperfection.

Write down one thing you've done recently that wasn't perfect but still moved you forward.

Keep it as a reminder that progress matters more than perfection.

FINAL TAKEAWAY

Forget perfect. Perfect is the enemy of your next breakthrough.

Aim for better.

Aim for consistency.

Aim for showing up—especially when it's hard.

Progress is still progress, even when it's not pretty.

Keep moving.

DAY 71

WHEN THE GRIND FEELS ENDLESS, KEEP GOING

Every man has hit that wall. The days when the weight feels unbearable. The mornings when even getting out of bed feels like a battle. The nights when doubt creeps in, whispering, Why are you even trying?

But strength isn't built on the days when everything clicks. It's forged in the moments when nothing makes sense—but you keep moving anyway.

RESILIENCE IS BUILT IN THE SILENCE

Think about the battles you've already faced. The ones that nearly broke you. The times quitting felt like the only option—but you didn't. You didn't have the perfect plan. You didn't have every answer. But you had fight.

And that fight? That's what separates the man who starts from the man who finishes.

We live in a world that glorifies results—but forgets the process. The highlights get all the praise. But real resilience? It's built in the quiet. In the nights when no one is watching. In the work that feels thankless. In the grind that feels endless. And still—you keep going.

ACTION CHALLENGE

Step 1: Focus on Today's Win.

Identify one small win you can create today.

Examples:

- Completing one task on your to-do list.
- Spending 10 minutes on a personal goal.
- Taking 5 minutes to reflect on why you started.

Step 2: Change Your Perspective.

Write down one thing you GET to do today instead of what you HAVE to do.

Examples:

- Instead of "I have to work late," say, "I get to show I can handle challenges."
- Instead of "I have to go to the gym," say, "I get to invest in my health."

FINAL TAKEAWAY

Small wins stack up. One step at a time. One choice at a time. Don't try to conquer the mountain—just keep moving forward.

You're stronger than you think.

And every day you don't quit?

That's proof.

DAY 72

YOU DON'T HAVE TO EARN REST – GIVING YOURSELF PERMISSION TO RECHARGE

Most men treat rest like something they have to earn. We tell ourselves, "I'll rest when I deserve it." "I haven't done enough yet." "There's too much to do—I'll slow down later."

But rest isn't a reward. It's a requirement.

THE MOMENT I REALIZED I HAD IT BACKWARD

For years, I believed rest was something you had to earn. I had to grind first. Hustle first. Prove myself first. And only when I'd done enough could I finally take a breath.

But what's "enough"? Because every time I hit a goal, I moved the target. Every box I checked only led to five more. And every time I thought about slowing down, I convinced myself I hadn't earned it yet.

Until my body made the call for me.

Burnout doesn't always show up as a crash. Sometimes, it's a slow fade—the kind you barely notice until everything feels heavy. The exhaustion that doesn't go away. The stress that lingers. The frustration that turns into resentment.

I had to learn the hard way:

If you don't give yourself permission to rest, life will force you to.

ACTION CHALLENGE

Step 1: Identify Your "Rest Guilt."

Think about the last time you felt guilty for resting.

Write it down.

Why did you feel guilty?

What made you think you hadn't "earned" it?

Step 2: Schedule Rest Like an Appointment.

Take out your calendar and block off one non-negotiable period of rest this week.

Examples:

- 30 minutes of doing nothing.
- A slow morning without checking your phone.
- An evening without working.

Then, when the time comes, protect it like you would a meeting with your boss.

FINAL TAKEAWAY

Rest isn't a break from progress—it's the fuel for it.

You don't have to earn rest.

You don't have to prove you're worthy of slowing down.

You just have to give yourself permission.

Not later.

Not when the to-do list is clear.

Now.

DAY 73

THE STRENGTH TO KEEP SHOWING UP

Some days, life doesn't just knock you down—it tries to bury you. You wake up drained, and by the time the sun sets, it feels like you've been running on fumes.

Everything feels heavier. Your patience wears thin. Your energy is gone. And the thought of pushing forward? Feels impossible.

But resilience isn't about pretending you're okay. It's not about forcing a smile or acting like the weight isn't crushing you. Real resilience is this—choosing to show up, even when you don't feel like it.

THE POWER OF SMALL, CONSISTENT ACTIONS

Think back to a time life hit you hard. Maybe it was a loss that shook you. A failure that made you question everything. Or a season where you felt stuck with no way out.

But you're still here. That's proof enough.

Resilience isn't about bouncing back in a day. It's about refusing to let life count you out.

We celebrate success like it's all about the big wins, but the real victories?

They happen in the quiet moments.

When no one's watching.

When you feel like you've got nothing left—but you show up anyway.

Those days—the ones where you don't quit—are the ones shaping the man you're becoming.

ACTION CHALLENGE

Step 1: Choose Your Anchor.

Identify one thing that can ground you today.

It could be a routine, a small win, or something that makes you feel like yourself.

Examples:

- Making your bed.
- Drinking a glass of water.
- Stepping outside for 5 minutes.

Write it down as a reminder of what's within your control.

Step 2: Show Up Anyway.

Choose one thing you've been avoiding—no matter how small—and take the first step toward it.

Examples:

- If you've been avoiding a conversation, send a message to open the door.
- If you've been procrastinating a task, spend 10 minutes working on it today.
- If life feels heavy, commit to doing one thing that restores you, like a walk or 5 minutes of breathing.

FINAL TAKEAWAY

Resilience isn't about never falling.

It's about rising—one more time than life knocks you down.

And you? You're still standing.

That's not just survival. That's strength.

PILLAR 5

FORGED IN THE FIRE

(DAYS 74–80)

You've stepped into your power. But power isn't just about action—it's about endurance. It's about holding your ground when everything around you is trying to shake you.

Nobody grows by staying comfortable. Nobody levels up by playing it safe. Real growth happens when you're stretched so far past your limits, you wonder if you can even take one more step.

It happens in the moments that feel like too much—when you feel exposed, challenged, and maybe even afraid.

But what are we taught as men? To hide it. To keep moving like nothing fazes us. We walk through fire and act like we don't feel the burn.

But ignoring the fire doesn't make you stronger. It just leaves you scorched.

That's why the challenge isn't just to keep moving. It's to face the fire, stand in it, and let it shape you instead of destroy you.

The world makes it easy to measure success by what people can see—a promotion, a new car, a bigger house. But the real growth? The kind that actually changes lives? It's the kind nobody claps for.

It's staying patient with your kids when frustration flares.

It's breaking cycles you were never taught how to escape.

It's healing wounds you never asked for, instead of bleeding on the people who love you.

You don't need applause to know you're growing.

Look at the choices you make, day after day. That's your proof.

Growth is messy. It's uncomfortable. And it rarely looks like success while you're in it. But men like you? You don't quit. You don't shrink. You keep showing up—even when it feels like no one notices.

And that? That's what makes you dangerous—in the best way.

So, ask yourself: Where are you right now? And where are you headed?

Not some flawless, filtered version of you.

I'm talking about the man you're becoming—right here, right now.

Because this isn't about chasing perfection.

It's about walking through the fire and coming out forged.

You've already been through things most people couldn't survive.

And you're still standing.

The scars you carry? They're not proof you failed.

They're proof you endured.

Every mistake. Every lesson. Every time you thought you'd break—and didn't.

That's your foundation. That's your evidence. You're built for more.

This is your moment. Not to change who you are—but to become more of who you were always meant to be.

The road ahead won't be smooth. It's not supposed to be.

But men like us? We don't need smooth roads.

We just need the will to keep walking.

DAY 74

SMALL MOVES, BIG SHIFTS

Getting started is usually the hardest part. You see the mountain ahead—whether it's the pressure of work, the weight of family responsibilities, or the personal dreams you've shelved for too long—and it feels impossible. You stare at it, waiting for the "right moment," but that moment never comes.

That's where most people get stuck—standing still, waiting instead of moving. But here's what I've learned: the right moment isn't something you wait for. It's something you create. Even the tallest mountain is climbed one step at a time.

THE POWER OF SMALL WINS

We've been conditioned to believe that progress has to be dramatic—big wins, overnight transformations, highlight reels and hustle culture. But that's a lie.

Life doesn't change through grand gestures. It's built in the small, unseen moments.

It's in showing up when quitting would've been easier. It's in choosing discipline over doubt. It's in taking one small action, even when you're tired, unsure, or afraid.

I know what it's like to feel like you're barely keeping your head above water. I've had days where just getting out of bed was the victory. At the time, it didn't feel like much. But looking back—those were the moments that saved me.

ACTION CHALLENGE

Step 1: Take the Smallest Step.

Write down one thing you've been avoiding—big or small.

Then, break it into a micro-action you can do today.

Examples:

- Instead of "clean the house," decide to organize one drawer.

- Instead of "fix my finances," commit to checking your account balance or setting up autopay.

- Instead of "improve my health," take a 5-minute walk or drink an extra glass of water.

Step 2: Track the Win.

At the end of the day, write down the small move you made and how it shifted your momentum.

FINAL TAKEAWAY

Small moves aren't small. They're the foundation for everything that follows.

Progress doesn't always shout. Growth doesn't always announce itself. But it's happening.

Keep going, even if it's slow. Because one day, you'll look back and realize that the quiet steps—the ones that felt invisible—were the ones that changed everything.

DAY 75

THE WINS THAT PROVE YOU'RE BUILT FOR THIS

When was the last time you gave yourself credit—not just a passing thought before moving on to the next thing, but a real moment to acknowledge how far you've come?

Most of us are wired to focus on what's still left to do. What's not done. What's not right. But today, slow down—not to look at what's ahead, but to recognize what you've already made it through.

THE STRENGTH IN LOOKING BACK

Think about it: You've had days when quitting felt like the easiest option. When the weight of life—work, family, pressure, expectations—made tapping out feel justified. But you didn't.

You kept going. You showed up. You handled responsibilities while running on fumes. You made moves that pushed you forward when staying stuck would've been more comfortable.

That's not just discipline. That's resilience. That's proof.

Proof that you've got what it takes.

Proof that you're built for more.

Proof that the man you're becoming is already in motion.

ACTION CHALLENGE

Step 1: Identify Your Hardest Win.

Look back on this journey and find one moment where you almost quit—but didn't.

Write it down.

- What made you push through?
- What did that experience teach you?

Step 2: Pass It On.

Call or message someone who's currently struggling—whether it's a friend, a family member, or a coworker.

Share what you learned from that moment and remind them they're built for more, too.

Step 3: Create a Personal Reminder.

Write one sentence about that win and place it somewhere visible—on your mirror, in your notes app, or as your phone wallpaper.

Let it be a reminder of your resilience when hard days hit again.

FINAL TAKEAWAY

You didn't just survive that season—you showed yourself who you are.

Don't minimize your wins. Use them.

Let them remind you. Let them refuel you.

Let them be the reason another man doesn't quit.

DAY 76

THE WINS THAT NO ONE CLAPS FOR

Everybody loves a highlight reel. Promotions. Weight loss transformations. New houses. Big wins. The kind of moments that get likes, applause, and attention.

But what about the days when you showed up even though no one was watching? When you got out of bed even though life felt heavy. When you kept your cool instead of snapping. When you chose discipline when no one would've blamed you for falling off.

Those moments? They count, too. Maybe more than you think.

THE POWER OF INVISIBLE WINS

It's easy to overlook the small victories because they don't come with fanfare. But ask yourself this: Where would you be right now if you hadn't taken those quiet steps forward?

Every strong man you admire—every story of success you've ever heard—it wasn't built on one massive moment. It was built in the trenches. On the ordinary days. In the moments that felt too small to matter, but stacked up to something meaningful.

Skipping over your small wins is like running a marathon and refusing to drink water at the mile markers. You'll burn out before you ever make it to the finish line.

ACTION CHALLENGE

Step 1: Recognize the Invisible Wins.

Think back over the past week and write down three "invisible" wins—

Moments when you showed up even though no one noticed.

Maybe you got through a hard day without snapping or you chose to do something good for yourself instead of giving in to old habits.

Step 2: End the Day with a 30-Second Gratitude Practice.

Say out loud, "I'm proud of myself for [insert win here]."

Make this a daily habit to train your mind to recognize your own progress.

FINAL TAKEAWAY

You're stacking bricks—even if the foundation isn't visible yet.

At the end of each day, name one win. Say it out loud. To yourself. Every day.

Because the man who learns to celebrate his own progress doesn't need a crowd to keep moving forward.

DAY 77

GRATITUDE IS YOUR STRENGTH IN MOTION

When was the last time you really sat with your progress—not just glanced at it, but actually let yourself feel it?

Not the "yeah, I guess I've come a long way" kind of thought, but a real, quiet recognition of what you've fought through to get here.

We spend so much time chasing what's next that we forget to honor what's now.

There's always another goal. Another thing to fix. Another version of "better."

But if you never stop to acknowledge what you've already overcome, you'll always feel behind—no matter how much you accomplish.

THE POWER OF LOOKING BACK

Think back to a time when you felt like you were at your limit.

Maybe you were drained—physically, emotionally, spiritually.

Maybe life hit so hard, you weren't sure you'd get back up.

But you did.

You found a way. Even if it wasn't graceful. Even if it took longer than you wanted.

That counts. That matters. That's something to be grateful for.

Gratitude isn't about pretending everything's been easy.

It's about recognizing that what you once prayed for, fought for, or thought would break you… is now part of the story that made you stronger.

ACTION CHALLENGE

Step 1: Write Down a Victory.

Think of a moment in your past when you thought you wouldn't make it—but did. Write down what that experience taught you and how it shaped the man you are today.

Step 2: Act on Gratitude.

Gratitude isn't just something you feel—it's something you show. Today, act on it.

Reach out to someone who's been there for you and tell them what that meant to you.

Acknowledge yourself—stand in the mirror and say out loud: "I'm proud of myself for making it this far."

Revisit a past struggle and remind yourself what it taught you. If you made it through that, what makes you think you can't handle what's ahead?

FINAL TAKEAWAY

You don't need to chase more to feel worthy.

Sometimes, you just need to pause and see what you've already built.

Gratitude isn't weakness.

It's fuel.

It reminds you of who you are—and pushes you toward who you're becoming.

DAY 78

THE GROWTH YOU DON'T SEE (BUT OTHERS DO)

When you wake up today, remind yourself of this:

The growth that matters most isn't always loud. Sometimes, it shows up in the smallest shifts—the silent wins no one else sees but you.

We've been conditioned to chase the big stuff: promotions, milestones, applause. But real transformation? That happens in the quiet. In the choices no one claps for. In the moments that don't make a post—but make you better.

THE STRENGTH IN SMALL WINS

Think back to a year ago. A month ago. Even just last week.

Have you changed?

Maybe not in a way that makes headlines—but what about the stuff only you would notice?

Maybe you held your temper when the old you would've snapped. Maybe you tackled something you've been putting off. Maybe you doubted yourself less today than you did yesterday.

That's growth. And it counts. Because the small wins? They stack.

ACTION CHALLENGE

Step 1: Create a "Small Wins" Log.

Grab a notebook or use your phone to start a list of the subtle wins you've had this week.

- Maybe it's showing patience in a tough situation.
- Maybe it's following through on something instead of pushing it off.
- Maybe it's just getting up and handling your business when you didn't feel like it.

Step 2: Ask for Feedback.

Reach out to someone you trust and ask them this:

"What's a way you've seen me grow or improve lately?"

Their perspective might highlight progress you haven't even noticed.

FINAL TAKEAWAY

Every time you choose progress—no matter how quiet—it lays another brick in the foundation of the man you're becoming.

Most men wait until the whole house is built before they give themselves credit.

But the men who keep rising?

They celebrate every brick they lay.

DAY 79

THE STRENGTH IN LOOKING BACK

When was the last time you really stopped to appreciate how far you've come?

Life moves fast. And as men, we're wired to focus on what's next—the next goal, the next problem to solve, the next person to show up for. But in the middle of the chase, we forget to pause. We forget to acknowledge the weight we've carried and the ground we've already covered.

THE POWER OF REFLECTION

Think back to the man you were when you started this journey. Maybe you felt stuck, overwhelmed, or unsure of yourself. Maybe you didn't have the clarity, the confidence, or the discipline you have now. Maybe you didn't even know how strong you really were.

Now think about the man you are today.

You may still be figuring things out—but look at how far you've come. You've faced setbacks and kept going. You've made decisions that scared you. You've learned things about yourself you never saw before. That alone is worth honoring.

ACTION CHALLENGE

Step 1: Reflect on a Victory.

Think back to a specific challenge that felt insurmountable at the time but that you overcame.

Write down:

- What happened?
- How did you feel in the moment?
- What did you learn from it?

Revisit this reflection whenever you need a reminder of your resilience.

Step 2: Create a Reminder.

Take a photo, save an object, or write a quote that represents your victory.

Keep it somewhere visible—on your desk, your phone's home screen, or in your wallet.

Let it serve as a tangible reminder of how far you've come.

FINAL TAKEAWAY

Too often, we measure success by how far we have left to go—when what we really need to do is honor how far we've already come.

Growth doesn't just live in the wins. It lives in the struggle.

In the quiet decisions to choose discipline over comfort.

In the moments you kept going when stopping felt easier.

Take a breath.

Be proud.

You've faced storms, carried burdens, and kept moving through it all.

That's not luck. That's who you are.

DAY 80
CLAP FOR YOURSELF FIRST

When was the last time you looked at yourself—not just in passing, not just to fix your collar—but really looked at the man in the mirror and respected him? Not for being perfect, but for pushing through when everything in you wanted to give up. For surviving the kind of days that would've broken the version of you from a few years ago.

THE PROBLEM WITH MOVING THE GOALPOST

Life doesn't slow down. Win something? Cool—what's next? Handle a crisis? Great—now fix the next fire. The goalpost keeps moving. And if you're not careful, you'll keep grinding without ever stopping to recognize the strength you've built.

That's how burnout sneaks in—not from weakness, but from never acknowledging the weight you've been carrying and still moving with.

Progress without recognition is like lifting heavier weights every day and never pausing to feel how strong you've become.

RESPECT THE MAN YOU'VE BECOME

You've been through storms most people don't even know about. You've fought battles behind closed doors. And yet, here you are. Not perfect. Not without scars. But still standing.

You won't always get applause for that. No one hands out trophies for personal growth. But the most important validation? It was never supposed to come from the outside anyway.

CELEBRATE THE WINS NO ONE SEES

We wait for the big milestones to celebrate. But your real growth came in the quiet victories. The days you showed up when you didn't feel like it. The moments you chose patience instead of pride. The times you stayed in the fight when walking away would've been easier.

FLIP THE SCRIPT

Stop waiting for someone else to acknowledge your progress. Be the one who sees it first. Don't just think about how far you've come—say it, write it, own it.

Maybe you responded better than you would've last year. Maybe you broke a generational pattern. Maybe you just kept going.

That deserves recognition.

ACTION CHALLENGE

Step 1: Record a "Self-Applause" Video.

Take 60 seconds to record yourself saying three things you're proud of.

Talk to yourself like you'd talk to a friend who's achieved something big.

Play it back anytime you feel like you're not making progress.

Step 2: Make a Commitment.

Write down one way you'll make self-recognition a habit going forward.

Examples:

- "Every Friday, I'll write down three things I did well this week."
- "When I reach a goal, I'll celebrate with [insert reward]."

FINAL TAKEAWAY

Make it a habit to clap for yourself—loudly and unapologetically.

When you do something hard, acknowledge it. When you grow in ways no one sees, make sure you see it. That's how momentum builds. That's how self-respect is rooted. That's how a man walks forward—knowing exactly who he is, and proud of it.

PILLAR 6

THE LEGACY YOU LIVE, NOT JUST LEAVE

DAYS 81–100

You don't build your legacy someday—you're building it right now.

Every conversation. Every decision. Every time you choose to show up or check out. You're shaping the story that will outlive you.

The question isn't whether you'll leave a legacy.

The question is: What kind of legacy are you living?

Legacy isn't about status or wealth. It's about the fingerprints you leave on people's lives. It's in how you guide your children. How you treat your partner. The lessons you pass down. The example you set—even when no one's watching.

Your legacy is how people feel when they think of you. It's the wisdom they carry because of you. The habits they inherit—for better or worse.

So ask yourself: When your name comes up—what will they say? Will they talk about the way you lifted them up—or the times you stayed silent? Will they carry forward cycles of strength—or cycles of struggle?

Legacy isn't just a reflection of what you leave behind.

It's a choice you make every day.

To build a legacy worth remembering, you need three things:

1. A VISION

Without a clear destination, life will pull you in every direction. Living on autopilot isn't leading—it's drifting.

What do you want your impact to be? What do you want to be remembered for?

A man with vision doesn't just react to life—he creates it.

2. VALUES THAT KEEP YOU GROUNDED

Life will test you. Without strong values, you'll get tossed around by whatever pressure comes your way. A man who stands for nothing falls for anything.

What do you stand for? What's the code you live by even when nobody's looking?

Your values are the roots that keep you steady when life tries to shake you.

3. VIRTUES THAT DEFINE YOUR ACTIONS

Your virtues are your internal compass—guiding how you treat people, how you handle pressure, and how you show up when it matters most.

Integrity. Resilience. Humility. Courage.

These aren't just ideals.

They're the bricks that build the kind of life that outlasts you.

Over the next few days, we're breaking this all down—what legacy really means, how to stop letting life push you around, and how to start building something that echoes long after you're gone.

This isn't about being perfect. It's about being intentional.

Because at the end of it all, it won't be about what you earned.

It'll be about what you built.

ONE LAST QUESTION:

What's one habit, one value, or one choice you can make today that moves you closer to the legacy you want to live—and leave?

DAY 81

THE WORK WAS NEVER JUST ABOUT 100 DAYS

Look at you. Eighty-one days deep. You've faced truths most men run from. You've taken steps that used to feel impossible. You've grown in ways you never could've imagined.

But let's be clear: this isn't the finish line. This is the turning point.

You didn't commit to this journey just to check off a goal. You started this because something in you knew there was more—a better life, a stronger mind, a deeper purpose.

And life? It's not impressed by milestones. It's going to keep testing you. Setbacks will still come. Doubt will still whisper. Hard days will still show up uninvited.

But the difference now? You're not the same man who started this.

You've got tools. You've got perspective. You've got the strength to face what used to break you.

You don't just survive anymore—you know how to stand. You know how to move through it.

Because this was never about reaching 100 days.

It's always been about how you show up after this.

How you carry what you've learned.

How you live what you've claimed.

ACTION CHALLENGE

Step 1: Write a Letter to Your Day 1 Self.

Be specific—what would you tell him about the growth you've experienced, the challenges you've overcome, and the lies about yourself that you've proven wrong?

Step 2: Write a Short Message from Your Future Self.

Imagine your Day 100 self speaking to you now. What advice is he giving you? Post this message somewhere visible—on your phone's lock screen, in your journal, or on your mirror.

This journey was never just about 100 days. It was about rewriting your story—one day at a time.

DAY 82

HOW TO KEEP GOING WHEN THE FIRE DIES DOWN

You know the feeling—that rush of energy when you start something new. When the possibilities feel endless. When you swear, this time will be different.

And then life steps in. The excitement fades. Distractions pile up. What felt urgent yesterday barely crosses your mind today.

That's when most people quit. Not because they weren't capable—but because they didn't prepare for this part of the journey.

THE REAL TEST ISN'T STARTING—IT'S STICKING WITH IT

Think about the goals you've started but didn't finish. The promises you made to yourself, then watched quietly slip away.

We've all been there. But this time can be different—because this time, you're not counting on motivation. You're choosing commitment.

Commitment isn't loud. It doesn't give you a rush.

It's quiet. Unshakable. Relentless.

It's waking up and doing the work, even when nothing in you feels like it.

It's moving forward when the progress is invisible.

It's trusting the process, even when the fire is nothing but a flicker.

ACTION CHALLENGE

Step 1: Build a "Reset Plan."

Think of one small but effective action you can take on the days you feel off-track.

Examples:

- Taking a five-minute walk to clear your mind.
- Journaling a quick gratitude list.
- Texting a trusted friend for accountability.

Step 2: Choose a Daily Anchor.

This is one habit you'll commit to no matter what (e.g., reading for 10 minutes, stretching in the morning, or writing down your daily goal).

Write it down. Schedule it. Make it non-negotiable.

FINAL TAKEAWAY

Your fire won't die because life gets hard.

It dies when you stop feeding it.

Keep showing up. Keep stacking days.

Because the men who finish are the ones who keep going through the quiet.

DAY 83

THE HABITS THAT KEEP YOU STRONG WHEN LIFE GETS HEAVY

Some men crumble under pressure. Others hold steady.

The difference? The habits they built before the storm hit.

YOUR HABITS EITHER GROUND YOU OR EXPOSE YOU

Most of us have tried to flip a switch and become someone new overnight. We go all in at the gym for a week, then fall off. Try to overhaul our entire routine in one shot, only to burn out. Make big promises to ourselves, but don't follow through.

That never lasts. Real change? It's built in the unseen, uncelebrated moments.

The days when you don't feel like showing up, but do anyway.

The mornings when you actually get out of bed when the alarm goes off.

The times you choose discipline over distraction.

That's what builds a man.

WHY SMALL HABITS MATTER MORE THAN BIG MOVES

Maybe you've started strong before, only to fall off when life got hectic. You're not alone. We've been conditioned to believe that going hard is the only way. But the truth is—consistency will take you further than intensity ever will.

It's not about how hard you push today. It's about how often you keep showing up.

It's not about grinding until you break. It's about pacing yourself to stay in the game.

ACTION CHALLENGE

Step 1: Pick One Habit That Feels Realistic but Impactful.

- Drinking a glass of water first thing in the morning.
- Journaling for three minutes.
- Taking five deep breaths before bed.

Start today.

Step 2: Track Your Habit for the Next Seven Days.

Use a sticky note, a calendar, or an app to mark each day you show up.

Seeing your progress builds momentum and reinforces consistency.

FINAL TAKEAWAY

Small steps, done consistently, will always outlast big leaps taken occasionally.

Growth isn't built through hype—it's built in the quiet, daily choices you make.

Keep showing up.

Even when it's hard.

Even when no one's watching.

That's how you win.

DAY 84

STAND ON WHAT YOU BELIEVE, EVEN WHEN IT'S HARD

Ever had a moment where you walked away from a situation and something just didn't sit right? Maybe you bit your tongue when you knew you should've spoken up. Maybe you went along with something that didn't sit right in your spirit.

That tightness in your chest? That quiet voice whispering, "You know better"?

That's your values telling you—you just stepped out of alignment.

THE TEST OF INTEGRITY

Life will test what you stand for. Every day, you'll be pulled in different directions—work, family, expectations, distractions. And if you don't have a clear anchor, it's easy to drift.

Your values aren't just a list in your phone or something you post on social media. They're the quiet choices you make when nobody's watching. The conversations you walk away from. The lines you refuse to cross. The peace you protect.

When you live by your principles, you don't have to over-explain. You don't have to defend or perform. You just move different—and that's real power.

Living with integrity won't always be easy. You might miss out on opportunities. You might be misunderstood. You might have to walk away from people who no longer fit the man you're becoming.

But that's the price of alignment—and it's always worth it.

ACTION CHALLENGE

Step 1: Define Your Non-Negotiables.

Write down three core values that you refuse to bend on. These are the anchors that guide your decisions.

Step 2: Reflect on a Moment of Compromise.

Think about a time in the last month when you compromised one of those values.

- Why did it happen?
- What stopped you from standing firm?
- What will you do differently next time?

FINAL TAKEAWAY

You don't need to be the loudest in the room. You don't need to argue your values into acceptance.

Just live them. Quietly. Boldly. Daily.

And let that be the legacy you leave.

DAY 85

SHARPEN THE TOOLS THAT WILL CARRY YOU FORWARD

Growth isn't something you check off a list. It's not a course you complete or a finish line you cross. It's a lifelong process—like building a toolkit you keep refining over time.

Every challenge, every stumble, every hard-earned lesson hands you something new—a tool you didn't have before.

THE QUIET WINS THAT BUILD YOU

Most of us don't stop to appreciate how far we've come. We're so locked in on the next goal, the next level, the next fire to put out that we overlook the quiet wins.

But take a second and look back. You've handled things this year that the old you would've folded under. You've shown patience in places that used to make you snap. You've started showing up for yourself in ways you once avoided.

That's growth. And it didn't happen by accident. That's the result of choosing to keep going, even when it was hard.

ACTION CHALLENGE

Step 1: Take Stock of Your Toolkit.

Write down three skills or strengths you've developed recently—patience, resilience, boundary-setting, or anything else.

Step 2: Put One to Work Today.

Choose one of those tools and apply it to a real situation.

Examples:

- If you've built discipline, tackle one task you've been procrastinating on.
- If you've learned to say "no", practice turning down a request that doesn't align with your priorities.
- If you've developed better communication skills, have a meaningful conversation where you actively listen instead of just waiting to reply.

FINAL TAKEAWAY

Growth isn't passive. It's built through intention—by using the tools you've earned to keep building the life you actually want.

You've already learned more than you give yourself credit for.

Now apply it. Sharpen it. Carry it forward.

DAY 86

THE MAN WHO STOPS GROWING, STOPS LIVING

Growth doesn't end. The moment you start thinking you've "arrived" is the moment you start drifting. Believing you've got it all figured out? That's one of the biggest lies a man can fall for.

Because life doesn't stop moving. It keeps shifting. Testing. Stretching. And the men who thrive are the ones who stay open, curious, and committed to growth—not just for themselves, but for the people who count on them.

THE TRAP OF THINKING YOU "KNOW ENOUGH"

There's this quiet pressure on men to have all the answers. To never slip. To never say, "I don't know." But real strength doesn't come from pretending. It comes from the humility to keep learning.

The strongest men are the ones who can say, "I don't have it all figured out—but I'm willing to show up, learn, and grow."

Think about the lessons that shaped you. Maybe you had to learn the hard way that pride can wreck a relationship. Or that patience can shift an argument into understanding. Those lessons didn't come easy— they came from staying open, owning your mistakes, and choosing growth over comfort.

ACTION CHALLENGE

Step 1: Identify One Area for Growth.

Write down one area of your life where you know you could grow.

Examples:

- Managing stress
- Improving communication
- Showing gratitude

Step 2: Take One Intentional Action Today.

For example:

- Read a chapter of a book that challenges your mindset.
- Ask someone you trust for honest feedback about an area you want to improve.
- Practice self-control by pausing before you react in a frustrating situation.

FINAL TAKEAWAY

Growth isn't always loud. It's not always some big breakthrough.

It's built in the quiet choices—the ones no one sees.

You don't need to have all the answers.

You just need to stay in the process.

The man you're becoming is built one decision at a time.

Don't wait until the timing is perfect.

Just move.

DAY 87

KEEP MOVING FORWARD—PROGRESS OVER PERFECTION

Ever have one of those days where it feels like life is passing you by? Like everybody else is hitting milestones, making moves, figuring things out—while you're just trying to keep your head above water?

It's easy to feel behind. Like you're running a race where the finish line keeps moving. But here's what you've got to remember: Your journey is yours. No one else has lived your story. No one's carried what you've carried. No one's fought your battles the way you have.

Progress isn't about keeping up with anyone else. It's about choosing to take one step forward—even when it's hard.

Some days, moving forward looks like winning. Other days, it looks like barely holding it together. But either way, you're still in the fight. And that counts for something.

THE STRENGTH IN SMALL STEPS

Think back to the moments when you felt like you had nothing left to give. Those nights when the weight in your chest felt unbearable. The days when doubt whispered, "You're not enough."

But you pushed through. And guess what? You're still here. That means something. That means you're stronger than you think.

Today, take a moment to honor that. You might not be where you want to be yet—but look at how far you've already come.

ACTION CHALLENGE

Step 1: Create a Momentum List.

Find one small thing that needs to be done today—a chore, an errand, an unfinished task. Complete it right now.

This isn't about the task itself—it's about creating momentum and proving to yourself that forward is forward, no matter how small.

Step 2: Track Your Steps.

At the end of the day, take two minutes to reflect:

- What are three ways you moved forward today?
- Maybe you showed up to work, handled a stressful situation calmly, or learned something new.

Write it down. Seeing it visually reminds you that progress is always happening.

FINAL TAKEAWAY

Progress doesn't always look pretty. But it always matters.

It's not about being perfect. It's about showing up—especially when it's hard.

Keep moving.

Keep stepping.

The man you're becoming is built by what you do today—not by how far you still have to go.

DAY 88

YOUR LEGACY IS NOW—STOP WAITING TO LIVE WITH PURPOSE

Most men don't think about their legacy until later in life—when the gray hairs start showing, when the kids are grown, when they finally slow down enough to ask, "Did I make any of this count?"

But legacy doesn't start at the end. It's happening right now.

In your choices. In your conversations. In the moments you decide to show up—or shrink back.

You're not waiting to write your story. You're writing it in real time.

LIVING WITH PURPOSE STARTS TODAY

Living with purpose isn't about making headlines or doing something the world applauds. It's about letting your daily life reflect the values you claim to stand on.

Think about the men who shaped you. Who really left their mark?

Was it the coach who pushed you harder when you wanted to quit?

The grandfather who never broke his word?

The big brother who showed up when no one else did?

Their impact didn't come from what they said. It came from how they lived.

Now it's your turn.

ACTION CHALLENGE

Step 1: Do a Legacy Audit.

Look at your calendar or to-do list for the past week.

- Identify one activity or meeting that didn't align with your values.
- Decide how you can adjust your time this week to prioritize what matters more.

Step 2: Teach Someone Something.

Think of one skill or piece of advice you can pass on to someone today.

Examples:

- Show your child how to tie a tie.
- Help a coworker with a task you've mastered.
- Share a lesson you've learned through experience.

Your legacy isn't built later—it's built now, in the moments you choose to be intentional.

FINAL TAKEAWAY

Legacy isn't something you leave behind.

It's something you live—right now.

You don't have to be perfect. But you do have to be present.

Don't wait for some distant future to live like you mean it.

Your legacy has already begun.

DAY 89

THE WEIGHT OF YOUR EVERYDAY CHOICES

Ever go through a day and wonder if any of it really mattered? Not the big moments—the everyday stuff. The way you answered the phone. The way you looked (or didn't look) at someone while they were talking. The tone in your voice when you walked through the door.

It's easy to think those little things don't count. But they do.

They add up.

YOUR DAILY CHOICES ECHO

The way you move through your day—it leaves a mark. Your daily choices aren't just habits. They're echoes. They ripple outward, shaping how people experience you, how they feel around you—and one day, how they'll remember you.

Think about someone who left a lasting impression on you. A teacher. A coach. A relative. Maybe it wasn't anything huge. Maybe it was how they always remembered your name. How they looked you in the eye. How they made everyone feel like they mattered—whether you were the CEO or the janitor.

The things that stick with us the longest aren't always the grand gestures.

It's the quiet consistencies. The small, repeated choices that say, "You matter. I'm present."

ACTION CHALLENGE

Step 1: Energy Audit Ritual.

At the end of today, take five minutes to mentally replay your interactions and activities.

Ask yourself:

- What gave me energy today?
- What drained me?

Write down one thing from each category.

Tomorrow, aim to increase the energy-giving activity and minimize the draining one.

This isn't about perfection—it's about gradually shifting your daily choices to align with what fuels you.

Step 2: The 1% Shift.

Pick one interaction you'll have today—whether it's with a family member, a coworker, or a stranger—and commit to showing up 1% more intentionally.

Examples:

- Add five extra seconds of eye contact.
- Offer a genuine compliment.
- Actively listen without distractions.

Step 3: The Reset Trigger.

Identify a moment today where your mood or focus shifts negatively—whether it's an argument, a moment of frustration, or feeling overwhelmed.

When it happens, use a reset technique:

- Take three deep breaths—count to four on each inhale and exhale.
- Physically change your position (stand up, step outside, stretch).
- Reframe the moment by silently asking, "How can I handle this in a way that aligns with the man I want to be?"

FINAL TAKEAWAY

The smallest moments leave the biggest marks. Your words. Your tone. Your presence. It all plants seeds—whether you notice or not.

So live like it matters.

Because it does.

Every day, you're becoming the man someone will remember.

Make that memory count.

DAY 90

YOU'RE NOT DONE—YOU'RE JUST GETTING STARTED

Look at you. Ninety days in. That's three months of showing up, pushing through, and choosing growth—even on the days when quitting would've been easier. If you've been waiting for someone to clap for you, go ahead and do it yourself. You earned this.

But let's be clear—this isn't the finish line. It's a checkpoint. The goal was never just to get here. The goal is to keep becoming.

The real question isn't, "What's next?" It's, "How do I make this who I am now?"

Growth isn't something you complete—it's something you commit to. You don't build a legacy by accident. It's not about titles, bank accounts, or applause. Legacy is how you show up when no one's watching. It's in the way you lead, the lessons you pass down, and how you handle pressure when life comes swinging.

So, look back at these 90 days. What shifted? Maybe you started facing yourself with more honesty. Maybe you stopped performing and started aligning with the man you want to be. Maybe—for the first time—you gave yourself permission to grow without shame.

Whatever it is, know this: these lessons weren't just for you. They're for everyone watching you—your kids, your brothers, your circle. The way you live going forward? It's going to give other men permission to grow too.

ACTION CHALLENGE

Step 1: Craft Your 10-Day Blueprint.

Take 10 minutes to plan the next 10 days. Write down:

- One theme or focus for the week (e.g., gratitude, consistency, or self-discipline).

- One non-negotiable habit you'll commit to daily (e.g., 10 minutes of reflection, morning exercise, or intentional presence with loved ones).

- One celebration trigger—a small way to reward yourself for sticking with it (e.g., a favorite coffee, a long walk, or quiet time).

Step 2: Create a Visual Reminder.

Choose one phrase or mantra that represents your commitment (e.g., "Keep building," "Consistency creates legacy," or "I'm in control of today"). Write it on a sticky note or make it the lock screen on your phone to keep it in front of you.

DAY 91

THE ENERGY YOU BRING SHAPES THE PEOPLE YOU LOVE

You might not always see it, but the way you move through the world changes the people around you.

The way you handle stress. The tone you set at home. The way you show up—or don't. It all creates ripples.

Most men are taught to carry things alone. To bottle it up. To push through and "deal with it later." But your silence leaves a weight. Your presence leaves an imprint. Your energy leaves a legacy.

HOW YOU SHOW UP MATTERS

Think about your role in the lives of the people closest to you. Whether you're a father, a partner, a brother, or a friend—your energy sets the emotional tone.

When you work on yourself, when you choose to respond instead of react, when you lead with intention instead of tension—you create room for the people you love to breathe, grow, and feel safe.

Now let's get real. Think about the last time you walked into your home after a hard day. Did your stress shift the whole atmosphere? Did your short answers shut down connection? Or did you take a moment to reset and choose to be present?

Those moments matter. They don't just affect you—they shape the environment you lead.

ACTION CHALLENGE

Step 1: The Energy Check-In.

Before you walk into your home or next interaction, pause.

- Take three slow breaths.
- Shake off the stress of the day.
- Mentally choose the energy you want to bring.

Step 2: The Three-Second Rule.

During your next conversation, count to three before responding—especially if you feel irritated or distracted.

Use the pause to remind yourself of the impact your tone and words have.

Step 3: The Recharge Ritual.

Find one simple action to reset your energy after a stressful moment.

It could be:

- A 10-minute walk.
- Sitting in silence with your favorite song.
- Deep breathing before engaging with others.

Your growth isn't just about you. It's a gift to the people who love you.

The legacy you leave isn't in what you say—it's in how you make people feel.

FINAL TAKEAWAY

Your energy is felt, even when you don't say a word.

When you show up with peace, you invite peace.

When you bring calm, others can exhale.

When you lead with love, everything shifts.

You don't need to be perfect—just intentional.

Because how you show up today becomes the emotional blueprint for tomorrow.

DAY 92

THE LEGACY YOU'RE LIVING RIGHT NOW

When most people hear the word legacy, they think of a name on a building, a fat bank account, or a long list of accomplishments. But legacy isn't just about what you leave behind—it's about how you show up while you're still here.

LOVE & INTEGRITY—THE FOUNDATIONS OF LEGACY

Legacy isn't built on money, titles, or status. It's built in the quiet, everyday moments. In how you speak to your partner after a long day. In how you show up when your child needs you. In how you respond when life tests your patience.

Integrity is doing the right thing when no one's watching. Love is choosing to show up—especially when it's inconvenient.

THE PEOPLE YOU IMPACT

Think back to a time when someone let you down. A father who wasn't there. A mentor who broke your trust. A friend who disappeared when you needed them most. Those moments stuck—not because of what they said, but because of how they made you feel.

Your legacy works the same way.

Most people won't remember every word you speak—but they'll remember the energy you carried. The way you made them feel. The presence you gave. Or didn't.

ACTION CHALLENGE

Step 1: The Gratitude Legacy.

Think of one person who has shaped your life in a meaningful way—whether they know it or not.

- Send them a quick message, call them, or write them a note letting them know how they impacted you.

Your acknowledgment doesn't just honor them—it reinforces the kind of legacy you want to live.

Step 2: Build a Legacy Ritual.

Identify one small habit or action you can practice daily to reinforce the legacy you want to live.

Examples:

- Start each day with a kind word.
- Commit to patience in tense moments.
- Dedicate five minutes to reflect on how you showed up.

Step 3: Pass It On.

Choose one piece of wisdom, a skill, or a value you want to pass on.

Examples:

- Teach your child how to tie a tie.
- Share a lesson with a coworker.
- Give advice to a friend.

FINAL TAKEAWAY

Your legacy isn't waiting on some future version of you.

It's happening right now.

Make sure the man you are today is building something you'll be proud of tomorrow.

Live your legacy.

Today. On purpose. With heart.

DAY 93

LIVE THE LEGACY YOU WANT TO LEAVE

One day, they'll talk about you. What do you want them to say?

Not just the job titles or the stuff you owned—but the real things. The things that make their voices crack when they speak your name. The moments that live in their bones, not just their memories. The stories your kids will tell—not because they have to, but because they can't forget the way you showed up, led with love, and left something real behind.

Legacy isn't just what you leave when you're gone. It's what you live every single day. And right now—today—you're writing that story with every choice you make.

As men, it's easy to get caught in the grind. We chase the next check, the next title, the next goal. And we push off the things that matter—being present, making memories, pouring into people—because we assume we have time.

But one day, "later" runs out.

Legacy isn't built in one big moment. It's built in the small, daily decisions—when you choose integrity over shortcuts, presence over performance, love over ego. It's in the way you show up when no one's watching. The lessons you pass down when no one else is teaching.

Don't just leave a legacy. Live it.

ACTION CHALLENGE

Step 1: Write Your Legacy Statement.

Take a moment to look at your life. What do you want your legacy to stand for? Maybe it's loyalty, honesty, or resilience. Maybe it's the love you showed in hard times or the way you refused to let life's punches make you cold and bitter. Write it down.

Be honest with yourself about the areas where you're falling short, but don't get stuck in guilt. See those gaps as opportunities to grow.

Step 2: Live It Today.

Pick one action that aligns with your legacy statement.

Examples:

- Have an intentional conversation with someone important to you.
- Model integrity in a decision, even if it's inconvenient.
- Show kindness to someone in a way that reflects the man you're becoming.

Today isn't just another day—it's another chance to live your legacy, not just leave one behind.

DAY 94

BE THE MENTOR YOU NEEDED

Think about the men who stepped in and shifted your life's direction. Maybe it was a father. Maybe it was a coach, an uncle, or an older brother figure—someone who saw something in you when you didn't see it in yourself.

They weren't perfect. But they dropped gems. They showed up when it mattered. And they gave you something solid to stand on.

Now it's your turn.

What kind of impact are you leaving for the ones coming behind you?

Being a mentor isn't about being flawless—it's about being real. It's about being present. About telling the truth, sharing your struggles, and passing down the lessons that would've saved you some scars if someone had told you sooner.

The most powerful mentoring moments rarely come with a heads-up. They show up in the quiet in-betweens—after a loss, on a long drive, in a quick check-in that turns into a breakthrough. Sometimes, it's just a sentence that lands when they needed it most.

ACTION CHALLENGE

Step 1: Drop the Lesson.

What's one lesson you had to learn the hard way? Write it down.

Then, pick someone in your life who needs to hear it—your son, nephew, mentee, or even a younger guy at work.

Step 2: Pass It On.

Reach out and share that piece of wisdom. This could be:

- A quick text: "I learned this the hard way, and I want you to have it before you have to."
- A conversation: "Man, let me tell you something I wish I knew when I was younger."

Mentorship isn't about getting credit. It's about paying forward the wisdom you wish you had sooner.

The world shifts when one man decides to invest in another, and that shift starts with you.

FINAL TAKEAWAY

You may not feel ready. You may not feel qualified.

But you know what you needed.

So now… be that man for somebody else.

DAY 95

THE MEN WHO BUILT YOU

When you think about the men who came before you—your father, grandfather, uncles, or even the men from your neighborhood—their fingerprints are all over your life, whether you realize it or not.

They left behind wisdom, sacrifices, and lessons—some spoken, many unspoken. Some gave you strength. Others left you with wounds. Some shaped you with their presence. Others shaped you with their absence.

But no matter how they showed up—or didn't—their choices helped mold the foundation you stand on today.

THE WEIGHT OF THEIR CHOICES

Maybe your father taught you what resilience looks like. Or maybe his absence taught you how to stand on your own. Maybe he built you up. Or maybe he became the reason you had to rebuild yourself.

But here's what matters: you're not just a product of their story. You're the author of what comes next.

Think about the sacrifices those men made. The ones you knew about—and the ones they took to the grave. Maybe they worked backbreaking jobs just to give their families a better shot. Maybe they fought battles—in war, in life, or within themselves—that you'll never fully understand.

Maybe they had dreams they had to bury, so you could have the freedom to chase yours.

And maybe—some of them didn't fight at all. Maybe they left you to figure it out on your own. And you did.

Honoring your legacy doesn't mean living in their shadow. And it's not about fixing what they couldn't.

It's about taking what they gave—the good, the bad, and everything in between—and deciding what you'll do with it.

You're a link in a chain. But you get to choose what kind of link you'll be.

ACTION CHALLENGE

Step 1: Honor or Heal.

Think of one man—your father, a mentor, a coach, a brother—who left a mark on your life.

Maybe he was your anchor, or maybe he was the storm you had to survive.

Maybe he built you up, or maybe he broke you down.

What did he teach you—intentionally or unintentionally?

How did his lessons—or his failures—shape the man you're becoming?

Write it down. Honor the good, learn from the pain, and decide how his story will shape the legacy you're building.

Step 2: Build on the Lessons.

Identify one strength or value you've inherited from the men before you (e.g., resilience, loyalty, or work ethic).

Decide one way you'll carry that forward starting today.

Example:

- "I'll show my resilience by not giving up on a goal I've been avoiding."

FINAL TAKEAWAY

Some men before you broke cycles.

Some men before you stayed stuck in them.

You get to decide what continues through you—and what ends with you.

DAY 96

THE LEGACY IN YOUR DAILY MOMENTS

One day, all that'll be left of you will be the stories people tell. What will they say? Will they talk about the way you showed up? The lessons you passed down? The little things that made them feel seen, safe, and valued?

Legacy isn't built in grand speeches or once-in-a-while efforts. It's built in the everyday moments.

The inside jokes you share with your kids. The way you always call your best friend on his birthday. The late-night talks with your partner that feel like home.

Traditions aren't just about holiday dinners or annual trips. They're the quiet, consistent ways you show love, lead with intention, and stay present. Those moments—more than anything else—will speak for you long after you're gone.

But here's the truth: you're already building traditions whether you realize it or not. The question is—are they the ones you want to be remembered for?

Do your daily actions reflect love, consistency, and presence? Or are you unintentionally passing down patterns of avoidance, emotional distance, or letting busyness take the lead?

Traditions are values in motion. If loyalty, kindness, and integrity matter to you, your habits should reflect that.

Your kids won't just remember what you said—they'll remember how you made them feel.

Your friends won't just recall your advice—they'll remember if you were the one who stayed when life got heavy.

Your legacy is being written right now—in the ordinary moments you think no one notices.

ACTION CHALLENGE

Step 1: Create a Tradition.

Choose one small tradition—a habit, a ritual, a gesture—that you can begin this week.

It could be:

- Sunday dinners where everyone puts their phones away.
- Writing your kids a note before a big test to remind them they're capable.
- Checking in on your people—not just when things are bad, but just because.

Traditions aren't about extravagance. They're about intention.

Step 2: Reflect and Adjust.

At the end of the week, reflect on how it felt to practice that tradition.

- What worked?
- What didn't?
- How can you make it sustainable and meaningful?

You don't need a special occasion to create meaning. Start today.

DAY 97

THE LEGACY YOU'RE LIVING RIGHT NOW

Most people think legacy is about what they leave behind. But legacy isn't just about what you leave—it's about how you live.

It's in how you treat people, even when no one's watching.

It's in how you show up when it matters.

It's in the way people feel after crossing paths with you.

Your words may fade—but your presence, your actions, your impact… those are what people carry forward.

One day, people will tell stories about you. What will they say?

Will they remember a man who was fully present?

Will they say you made them feel seen, encouraged, protected?

Will they say you led with integrity, even when it cost you something?

Here's what most men don't realize: you don't get to choose whether you leave a legacy.

You only get to choose what kind you leave.

ACTION CHALLENGE

Step 1: Identify Your Living Legacy.

Think about one way your daily actions are already shaping your legacy.

- Do people see you as someone who keeps their word?
- Do you make others feel safe, encouraged, or inspired?
- Or are you letting busyness and distractions keep you from being present?

Step 2: Take One Intentional Action Today.

Decide on one way you will reinforce the legacy you want to live.

- Call someone who needs to hear your voice.
- Follow through on a promise, even if it's small.
- Show up today in a way that makes someone's life better.

FINAL TAKEAWAY

Your legacy isn't in what you say—it's in how you show up. Every day, you're writing your story. The question is: Is it one you'd be proud to pass down?

Your life is your message.

Make it one worth remembering.

DAY 98

YOUR INFLUENCE SPEAKS LOUDER THAN YOU KNOW

You may not see it, but someone is watching you right now.

A younger sibling paying attention to how you handle pressure. A coworker learning from how you carry yourself. A friend quietly taking notes on how you show up when things get hard. You're influencing people—even when you don't realize it.

Every choice you make—how you respond to setbacks, how you treat others, how you carry yourself when life gets heavy—is shaping how someone else sees leadership, strength, and character.

THE INFLUENCE YOU DON'T ALWAYS NOTICE

Think about a time someone impacted your life—and they didn't even know it. Maybe it was a mentor, a coach, a friend. Maybe it was a single conversation that stayed with you for years. Maybe it was just someone who believed in you when you didn't believe in yourself.

That's influence.

And whether you see it or not, you're doing the same for someone else right now.

WHO'S WATCHING YOU RIGHT NOW?

We often think leadership is about titles, money, or recognition. But real leadership? It's how you show up when no one's clapping. It's who you are when no one's keeping score.

You don't have to be famous to leave a mark. You just have to be consistent.

Are you the kind of man whose presence makes people better? Are you living in a way you'd be proud for your son, your brother, or your younger self to follow?

Because one day, someone will tell their story—and your name will be in it.

What will they say?

ACTION CHALLENGE

Step 1: Acknowledge the Influence in Your Life.

Think of one person who has influenced you in a meaningful way.

- Maybe it was a mentor, a coach, or a friend.
- Maybe it was someone who simply believed in you when you didn't believe in yourself.

Send them a message, give them a call, or tell them in person what their presence meant to you.

Step 2: Recognize Who's Watching You.

Think about who in your life might be silently learning from you.

- Who's watching how you handle stress?
- Who's picking up on how you treat others?
- Who will one day tell a story about the impact you had on them?

Your influence is already shaping lives. Own it.

FINAL TAKEAWAY

Your loudest impact isn't made with a mic—it's made with your life.

You don't need a stage to lead. Someone is learning from you right now.

Make the lesson worth remembering.

Live like it matters.

Because it does.

DAY 99

THE MARK YOU LEAVE BEHIND

One day, all that will be left of you is the stories people tell.

Will those stories be about how you lifted others—or how you stayed silent when it mattered most?

Every man leaves a mark. But not every man leaves the right one. And it's not just in the big moments. Not just in what you build, earn, or accomplish. It's in how you live—every single day.

You may not see it yet, but your presence, your words, your choices—they're shaping how people will remember you. The way you treat others when no one's watching. The way you respond to pressure when life hits hard. The way you love, lead, and show up for the people who need you.

Because at the end of it all, no one's going to talk about how much money you made. They won't care about the titles or the status.

They'll remember how you made them feel.

THE QUIET LEGACY YOU'RE ALREADY CREATING

Think about a time when someone's presence shifted something in you. Maybe it was a mentor who saw something in you you couldn't yet see. Maybe it was a father figure whose consistency spoke louder than words. Maybe it was a stranger whose kindness reminded you there's still good in the world.

That's impact. That's legacy. And now—it's your turn.

Because whether you realize it or not, you're already leaving a mark. The only question is: Are you shaping it with intention—or letting it be written by default?

ACTION CHALLENGE

Step 1: Write Your Legacy in One Sentence.

If someone had to sum up who you were and what you stood for in one sentence, what would you want them to say?

Examples:

- "He was a man who made people feel seen."
- "He never broke his word."
- "He lifted others every chance he got."

Step 2: Take One Action to Reinforce It.

Now, do something today that matches the legacy you want to leave.

- If you want to be remembered as a man of integrity, keep your word—no matter how small.
- If you want to be remembered as a man who made people feel valued, take time to acknowledge someone today.
- If you want to be remembered as a man who led with love, show up for someone who needs you.

FINAL TAKEAWAY

You don't have to be famous to be unforgettable.

Your name will be spoken long after you're gone—make sure it's for the right reasons.

The impact you make today will outlive you. Make it count.

You're writing your story with every breath.

Make sure it's one worth telling.

DAY 100

HOW TO KEEP GOING WHEN THE FIRE DIES DOWN

This isn't the end of the journey. This is the moment you decide whether everything you've learned becomes your lifestyle—or just another thing you started but didn't finish.

You've made it to Day 100.

But let's be clear: this isn't the finish line. This is where the real work begins.

Growth doesn't stop here. You don't go back to who you were.

You've challenged yourself. You've questioned old beliefs. You've built new habits. You've faced your past and stepped into a new way of living.

But the hardest part?

Staying consistent.

Because life will keep coming. The doubts will creep in. The world will test you. Old habits will call your name.

But this time? You're not the same man who started this.

This time, you know who you are.

This time, you've got tools.

This time, you've got receipts.

YOUR LEGACY IS BUILT IN THE DAILY CHOICES

Every decision from here on either strengthens the man you're becoming—or pulls you back into who you used to be.

When the fire starts to fade, remember what lit it.

When the weight gets heavy, lean on what you've built.

When the people around you don't understand, lead anyway.

You weren't made to live on autopilot. You weren't built to just survive. You were born to move boldly. To build something that outlives you. To rise higher than you ever thought possible.

FINAL CHALLENGE
MAKE A COMMITMENT TO YOURSELF

Step 1: Write down one commitment for the next 100 days.

And then? Do it today. Don't wait. Don't plan. Just take action—right now.

Step 2: Take One Bold Action Today.

- Call the person you've been meaning to reconnect with.
- Follow through on something you promised yourself you'd do.
- Step into a challenge you've been avoiding.

Prove to yourself that this wasn't just a book you read—this is a life you're living.

FINAL TAKEAWAY

You didn't come this far just to stop here.

This isn't the end.

It's the beginning of everything you were built for.

You don't wait for the right moment.

You create it.

You've laid the foundation.

Now go build the life.

CONCLUSION

THE BROTHERHOOD YOU BUILD

By now, you know—this journey was never just about you. Real growth isn't just measured by how far you've come, but by who you bring with you.

As men, we've got to check our egos when it comes to that. I've seen it firsthand—women have built powerful communities where they show up, uplift each other, and grow together. They don't just talk about support—they live it.

But us? We say we want that. We say we need it. But when it's time to commit? We disappear. Why? Because we're busy? Tired? Too caught up in our own world?

Nah. We make time for what matters. And this—this matters.

Brotherhood isn't extra. It's essential. It touches every area of your life. It makes you a better father, a stronger partner, a more grounded leader. It's about having men around you who don't just nod and say, "Yeah, I feel you"—but challenge you, hold you accountable, and remind you of who you are when you forget.

If you don't have that kind of circle yet, start building it. Start small. One man. One real conversation. Be the one who reaches out. Check on someone who's struggling. Be present. Ask better questions. Call instead of just texting.

Brotherhood isn't about a title, a group, or a membership. It's about the men who show up in the fight with you—and for you.

Let's be clear: no one's coming to save you. But that doesn't mean you have to do this alone.

So, let's do better. Let's stop saying we want it and start being it. Build your circle. Be the man another man can count on.

YOUR NEXT CHAPTER STARTS NOW

That man who wasn't sure if he could do this? That man is you. And he was never weak—he was just waiting on the moment to step fully into his power.

This journey hasn't been easy. It made you confront what you've buried, what felt too heavy to carry, too painful to face. But you didn't run. You didn't numb out. You didn't shrink.

You stood in the fire. And you let it shape you.

Society will try to define your worth by your paycheck, your status, or what you can provide. But let's set the record straight: your worth isn't in what you earn—it's in how you show up. It's in the way you love. The way you lead. The way you rise after you fall.

These past 100 days weren't about being perfect. They were about peeling back the noise, shutting out the lies, and remembering who you are.

But this isn't the end.

Because real change? It doesn't come from finishing something—it comes from showing up again and again for the life you're building.

The foundation is set.

Now it's time to build.

The foundation is set.

Now, it's time to build.

YOUR CHARGE: KEEP MOVING, KEEP BUILDING, KEEP RISING

With every decision, every act of courage, you're writing the next chapter of your life. And you're not writing it alone. There's a brotherhood of men walking this same path—breaking cycles, leading with heart, and standing in truth.

You are part of something bigger than you. And when you rise, you don't just lift yourself.

You lift your family. Your community. Your legacy.

So when life gets heavy—and it will—come back to these pages. Let them remind you who you are and who you're becoming. A man who leads with heart. A man who stands firm in his values. A man who refuses to live on autopilot.

You didn't come this far just to come this far.

So keep going.

STEP FULLY INTO THE LIFE THAT'S WAITING FOR YOU

This is your charge: Step fully into the life you were built to live.

The work you've done has prepared you for this moment.

No more waiting. No more shrinking. No more second-guessing.

Now—walk boldly.

Build your legacy.

Live wide awake.

This isn't the end.

It's the beginning—of a bigger, bolder, more intentional life.

And the only way to live it is forward.

Growth doesn't happen in a vacuum.

It happens in the daily choices you make to keep going—even when it's not easy.

Here's how to stay sharp, stay grounded, and keep rising:

OWN YOUR MORNINGS, OWN YOUR MINDSET

Start your day with intention—not distraction.

Before you reach for your phone or scroll your timeline, check in with yourself:

- What's one thing I can do today to move forward?
- How can I show up as the man I want to be?
- Where do I need to step up—or let go?

Your mornings shape your mindset.

Reflection keeps you grounded and in control.

SET YOUR NEXT 100-DAY VISION

The last 100 days shaped you. Now it's time to go further.

What do you want to build, change, or pursue over the next 100?

Set three goals that stretch you.

Break them down.

Take action.

And don't stop until you cross that finish line.

LOCK IN YOUR CIRCLE

You don't grow strong alone. You need men in your corner who will check you, challenge you, and cheer for you.

If you don't have a circle—build one.

Start with one honest conversation. Be the one who reaches out.

REVISIT THE HARD DAYS

When doubt creeps in—and it will—come back to these pages.

Let them remind you of:

- What you've already overcome
- Why you started

Progress isn't always pretty. But every step counts.

Keep walking.

LEAD FROM WHERE YOU ARE

Your growth isn't just for you. Someone out there needs what you've learned.

Whether it's your son, your brother, your friend, or someone you haven't even met yet—be the man who shows up, speaks truth, and lifts others higher.

KEEP YOUR MIND & BODY RIGHT

Your body is your foundation. Treat it like it matters.

Move every day.

Fuel yourself with intention.

Protect your peace.

Rest without guilt.

A strong man isn't just mentally sharp—he's physically ready for whatever life throws his way.

BET ON YOURSELF, ALWAYS

You've already proven you can do hard things.

Now it's time to dream bigger.

Move with purpose.

And go after the life that's been waiting on you to believe.

No more playing small.

No more waiting for the "right" moment.

It's your time.

FINAL WORD THIS IS JUST THE BEGINNING

You didn't come this far to stop here.

This isn't the end.

It's the beginning— of everything you were built for.

You don't wait for the right moment.

You create it.

You don't need permission.

You walk in it.

Because one day,

someone will tell their story…

and your name will be in it.

Make sure they say:

"He changed my life."

Now close this book.

And go live the one you were born for.

ACKNOWLEDGEMENTS

FAITH & FOUNDATION

First and foremost, I thank God—for the vision, the strength, and the perseverance. This book was placed on my heart in December 2023, and here we are in February 2025. Through every challenge and every moment of doubt, He never let me shake the calling to finish it. No matter what was going on, He kept putting it in my spirit: This book has to be written. And now, here it is.

To my wife, Nisa—the best thing that ever happened to me. You've supported me in ways I can't even put into words. You believed in me when I struggled to believe in myself. When I was tired, overwhelmed, and ready to walk away from writing to "just get a job," you wouldn't let me. You saw the impact I was making, even when I couldn't. I wouldn't be the man I am without you, and I wouldn't have finished this book without your love, your patience, and your unwavering belief in me.

To my sons, Ahmad and Anthony Jr.—my greatest motivation. Every single day, you push me to be a better man, a better father, and a better example. You remind me what legacy truly means. It's not about what I leave behind—it's about what I pour into you while I'm here.

To my younger brother, Tyreese—you were the first person who made me want to be better. I wanted to be the role model we never had. In striving to be that, you helped shape who I became.

To my mother—you always told me I could do anything. I know it wasn't easy being a young, single Black mother. I know you carried more than you ever let me see. But because of you, I never doubted I could be more, do more, and create more. Your strength made me who I am. Thank you for every sacrifice, every lesson, every push toward greatness.

To my granny—the woman who gave me my first foundation in faith, family, and service. You made sure I had the tools to succeed—not just in school or work, but in life. Your strength and belief in me live on in these pages. This book is your legacy too.

To my grandfather, Willie "Sarge" Jones—the only consistent male role model I had growing up. Your quiet strength and steady presence taught me what it means to show up. Thank you for giving me a standard to look up to.

To my father, who wasn't there—there was a time I carried anger for your absence. But I've made peace with it. Even without being present in my life, you still shaped me. I forgive you, and I pray you've found peace. Whatever strength or resilience is in me—I believe some of it came from you. For that, I thank you.

BROTHERS FOR LIFE

To my best friend, Travis—my brother in every way that matters. We grew up figuring life out together, and no matter how close or far we were, you always had my back. That kind of loyalty is rare, and I'll always be grateful for it.

To Dr. Mahdi "Mark" Brown—you're like a brother to me. From the moment we met in college when you were my RA freshman year, to now, no matter where you are in the world, we've always stayed connected. We've supported each other through life, business, and every phase of growth. You're Anthony Jr.'s godfather for a reason—your presence in my life has been invaluable. Thank you for being family in every way that counts.

To my college brothers—Crew Love. We became men together. We've been through a lifetime's worth of experiences: growth, loss, joy, pain, transitions, and wins. And nearly 30 years later, we're still standing strong. That kind of bond can't be broken. Thank you for walking with me through it all. Y'all are part of my foundation too.

COUSINS, SIBLINGS, & FIRST ROLE MODELS

To Mike—you were like a big brother from the start. If you did it, I wanted to try it too. Baseball, hoop, music—you led, and I followed. I remember playing around with your keyboard and falling in love with creating sounds. You were the first person to visit me at college and the only one who showed up to my graduation. I never told you how much that meant to me, but I felt it. You always looked out for me, even when I didn't know how to ask for it. That's love. And I'll always be thankful.

To Rick—solid, always. You didn't have to show up the way you did, but you did. You introduced me to music in a way that helped shape my creativity. More than that, I watched how you carried yourself, how you cared for your family. I learned from that. I respect the man and father you've become. I'm proud to call you brother.

To my cousin and big sister, Cureston—we fought as kids, but now I understand: you love hard. And you've never stopped being that for me and my family.

To my younger cousins—I just wanted to be the example. The first to do certain things so you could see what was possible. I hope I've inspired you to see the greatness in yourselves.

To my cousin Antwan—this is dedicated to you. You may be gone physically, but your spirit is always with me.

To my amazing aunts—thank you for helping raise me, for loving me in the way only family can. I carry your encouragement with me always.

PROFESSIONAL PARTNERS & LIFELONG SUPPORTERS

To my former publicist, business partner, and co-author of my children's book, Kristy—thank you for helping get my first book into the world. Your early support made an impact I'll never forget.

To my current publicist, Jennifer—thank you for being a steady presence as I finished this project. For helping put my books in the hands of people who need them. For opening doors to companies, organizations, and communities I once only dreamed of reaching. But most of all, thank you for your friendship, consistency, and belief in me.

TO MY EXTENDED FAMILY & THOSE WHO SUPPORTED ME FROM DAY ONE

To my social media family—the friends, brothers, and sisters I've met through this work. Some of you have been with me since before I ever called myself an author. Before I believed my words mattered. You didn't just watch me grow—you helped me grow. And I'll always be grateful for that.

To anyone I may not have named by name, but who's been part of this journey—I see you. I appreciate you. I thank you.

FINAL WORDS

This book is bigger than me. It's a reflection of every person, every moment, and every lesson that helped shape me. And for that—I'm forever grateful.

ABOUT THE AUTHOR

ANTHONY D. BRICE

Anthony D. Brice is a bestselling author, transformation coach, and one of today's leading voices in self-empowerment and personal growth. His words reach hundreds of thousands daily, inspiring people to break cycles, embrace their worth, and rise into the lives they were meant to live.

Through books like Poor Me to Soul Rich and In Her Hour of Need, Anthony shares raw, practical insights on healing, resilience, and personal transformation. His writing confronts outdated narratives—especially around masculinity, emotional intelligence, and self-worth.

Anthony's approach is grounded and real. He doesn't preach perfection—he champions presence, purpose, and the courage to show up every day. His mission is simple: help men and women reclaim their power, rewrite their stories, and build lives rooted in confidence, authenticity, and impact.

Want to stay connected? Join the movement.

- Instagram: [@anthonydbrice]
- TikTok: [@anthonydbrice]
- YouTube: [@anthonydbrice]
- Website: [anthonydbrice.com]

Keep growing. Keep building. Keep rising

www.ingramcontent.com/pod-product-compliance
Lightning Source LLC
Chambersburg PA
CBHW020454030426
42337CB00011B/112